I0007853

VB.NET CODE WARRIOR

Working with Access

By Richard Thomas Edwards

*This is the Dedicated to all my friends I left behind and
never got a chance to say goodbye.*

CONTENTS

THE PURPOSE OF THIS BOOK

You can learn a lot in a short time when you have the basics
that you know already works.
—R. T. Edwards

When I started working on this book, I thought I had a pretty good handle on what I knew I could or couldn't do with Access. After all, I did work for Microsoft in Technical Support between 1996 and 2002 and many of the issues I worked on were dealing with Access 2, 95, 97 and 2000. But today's Office 365 is a beast! It has more horsepower and more bells and whistles than ever before!

But not all of Access's enhancements are Internet "tribal knowledge".

In fact, I can promise you that some solutions will be found only here because a lot of the issues are being caused by Microsoft's once respected MSDN – on or not on purpose – that just do not work, are vague, misleading and have code examples that are VB.Net prejudicial – they are written for Powershell, C# or C++.Net.

Why in the world would a company who has devoted the last 25 years to using the Component Object Model (COM) not want to embrace languages and encourage the use of Perlscript, VB.NET, Rexx and Ruby. If the excuse is that they think these languages should go away, they aren't any time soon - which was one of my many reasons why I chose to learn VB.NET in the first place. After all, languages were built to address a problem or groups of problems that couldn't be solved using existing and popular programming languages.

What I'm about to cover is the newest version of Access: Access 365; and, hopefully amaze you with brilliant solutions you won't find on the web.

SO WHY AN E-BOOK ON ACCESS

Better than an out of the box experience.

*Knowing what is possible and what you are capable of, makes
you a code champion.*
—R. T. Edwards

Let's face it, out of the box solutions are boring often supplied to fuel your imagination. Unfortunately, many programmers just don't have the time to spend learning how and why the pieces of the puzzle do, indeed, work with each other to generate something bigger and better than the program was designed to do out of the box.

My goal here is to take work out the kinks – so to speak – and supply you with the solutions and the work arounds. The result: saving you time effort and tons of frustration in the process.

SO, WHAT IS SO GREAT ABOUT THE DOM

Master the DOM, save the world.
—R. T. Edwards

L isten, I don't plan on making you an overnight success But if you've gotten this far into this book, then what I'm about to cover will make up for all the time you have spent so far to get here. Imagine for a moment, having to write code blindfolded.

Wouldn't be easy, would take a lot longer to do and you probably wouldn't get paid much in the process. Well, the DOM is like your eyes into the object that you create in code. And in the case of Access it is a rather large inventory of things to do and stuff to add to your VB.NET code.

For example, you go up to the web and they tell you that using Access.Application, you can write the following to create an Access database:

```
Dim oAccess As Object = CreateObject("Access.Application")
oAccess.NewCurrentDatabase(DBName, 9) #For an Access 2000
database
```

```
Dim oAccess As Object = CreateObject("Access.Application")
oAccess.NewCurrentDatabase(DBName, 10) #For an Access 2002
```
database

```
Dim oAccess As Object = CreateObject("Access.Application")
oAccess.NewCurrentDatabase(DBName, 12) #For an Access 2007
```
database

```
Dim oAccess As Object = CreateObject("Access.Application")
oAccess.NewCurrentDatabase(DBName, 0)  #For creating a
```
Default Access database

Furthermore, not all the DOMs for the various versions of Access are the same. For example – I believe it is the Access DOM for 2007 – which also had support for Access 2, Access 95 and Access 97 – would have allowed you to do all the above and these three:

```
Dim oAccess As Object = CreateObject ("Access.Application")
oAccess.NewCurrentDatabase(DBName, 1)  #For an Access 2
```
database

```
Dim oAccess As Object = CreateObject("Access.Application")
oAccess.NewCurrentDatabase(DBName, 7)  #For an Access 95
```
database

```
Dim oAccess As Object = CreateObject("Access.Application")
oAccess.NewCurrentDatabase(DBName, 8)  #For an Access 97
```
database

But that is not as important as the fact that the compatible DAO suggests some other rather important and interesting database creation formats of its own:

```
dbVersion10    1
dbVersion11    8
dbVersion20    16
dbVersion30    32
dbVersion40    64
dbVersion120  128
dbVersion140  256
dbVersion150  512
```

Only problem is, these additional versions are not in COM. In fact, the COM or Component Object Model engine installed on the machine I am typing this on is DAO.DBEngine.120. I seriously doubt that you're going to get dbVersion140 or dbVersion150 out of DAO.DBEngine.120.

But this book isn't about DAO. That will get covered in a different E-book. Right now, we're going to be dealing with Access and the Access.Application object we can call from COM.

ANOTHER CRITICAL SUBJECT

The Import\export functionality in Access

Never assume you think you know how to do something. When you don't, it will bite you in the butt every time.
—R. T. Edwards

T he first thing you need to know about this is I am taking what I know about it and fixing an issue that even Microsoft's MSDN's explanation of it is so misleading that you couldn't possibly get it to work. Please, look at the following code:

```
Dim l as Object = CreateObject("WbemScripting.SWbemLocator")
Dim svc as Object = l.ConnectServer(".", "root\\cimv2")
svc.Security_.AuthenticationLevel = 6
svc.Security_.ImpersonationLevel = 3
Dim ob as Object =  svc.Get("Win32_Product")
Dim objs as Object =  ob.Instances_
```

```
Dim oAccess As Object = CreateObject("Access.Application")
oAccess.NewCurrentDatabase("D:\Products.accdb", 0)
Dim db As Object = oAccess.CurrentDB()
Dim tbldef as Object =  db.CreateTableDef("Product_Properties")
For each obj in objs
   For Each prop in obj.Properties_
      Dim fld As Object = tblDef.CreateField(prop.Name, 12)
      fld.AllowZeroLength = True
      tbldef.Fields.Append(fld)
   Next
   break
Next

db.tableDefs.Append(tbldef)

Dim rs As Object = db.OpenRecordset("Product_Properties")
For each obj in objs
   rs.AddNew
   For Each prop in obj.Properties_
     n= prop.Name
     rs.Fields(n).Value = GetValue(n, obj)
   Next
   rs.Update
 Next
```

When this code is finished it will create an Access Database with an accdb file extension.

But suppose I wanted to Export the file into a text file?
If could write the following:

```
Dim cn As Object = CreateObject ("ADODB.Connection")
```

```
cn.ConnectionString ="Provider=Microsoft.Jet.OLEDB.4.0;Data
Source = D:\Process.accdb;"
cn.Open

cn.Execute("Select * INTO[Text; hdr=yes; Format=CSVDelimited;
Database=D:\].[Process_Properties.csv] From [Products]")
```

Or, I could do this:

```
Dim oAccess As Object = CreateObject("Access.Application")
oAccess.OpenCurrentDatabase("D:\Process.accdb")
oAccess.DoCmd.TransferText 2,"","Process_Properties",
"D:\Process1.csv",1, ,437
```

All well and good but what happens if I don't want a CSV file
format? Perhaps a tilde or Exclamation?

As it turns out, there is a bit of Magic you do.

Start Access, open the database you want to use for exporting,
highlight the table you want to export and then right click it.

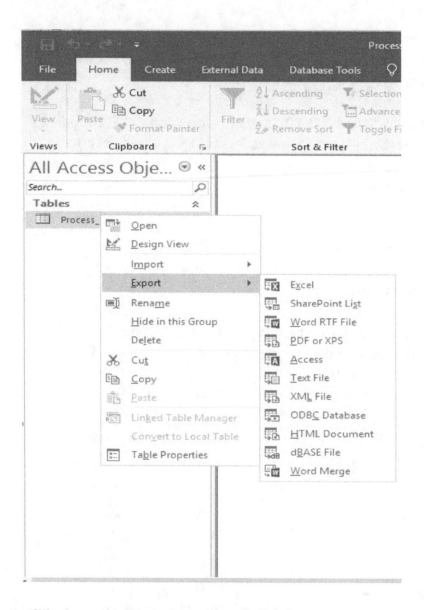

Slide down the list to Text File and click it.

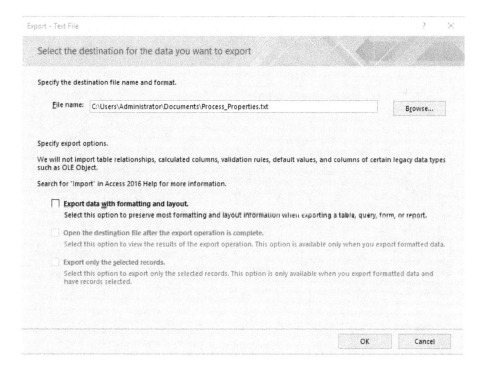

Other than placing the file in a different location besides the default location, click Okay.

If you select the Export data with formatting and layout, you will not get to the next important step. Change the location, leave everything else alone.

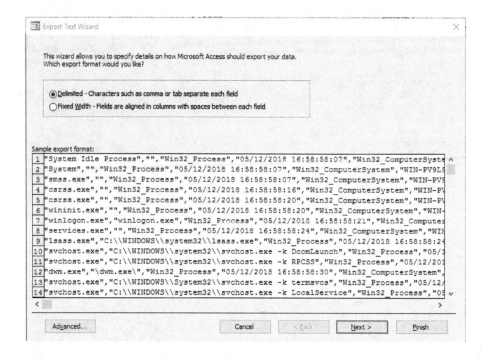

If you've worked with Excel before, this might look kind of familiar. Anyway, the next step is to click on the Advanced button on the left.

That will bring you to where you master the craft of importing and exporting.

Process_Properties Export Specification

| File Format: | ⦿ Delimited | Field Delimiter: | , ∨ | OK |
| | ○ Fixed Width | Text Qualifier: | " ∨ | Cancel |

Language: English ∨

Code Page: Western European (Windows) ∨

Save As...

Specs...

Dates, Times, and Numbers

Date Order: MDY ∨   ☑ Four Digit Years

Date Delimiter: /   ☐ Leading Zeros in Dates

Time Delimiter: :   Decimal Symbol: .

Field Information:

| Field Name |
| Caption |
| CommandLine |
| CreationClassNan |
| CreationDate |
| CSCreationClassN |
| CSName |
| Description |
| ExecutablePath |
| ExecutionState |

First, change the delimiter in the Combo box right beside the Field Delimiter label. Do not click okay. Instead, click on the Save As button. The program will go through the list of field names and create an input dialog where you can change the name pf the Specification file.

Either write it down the name provided or change it to a name you want to use.

Click okay.

Congratulations! You now have your specification file Name!

Now, click the okay.

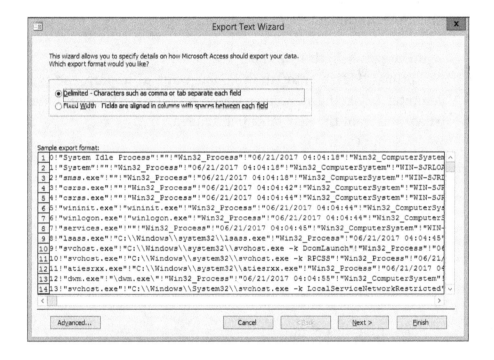

Notice the delimiter you selected has replaced the comma . The file will be created after you click finish.

You have now created your first custom delimited file.

The problem as I see it is all of this is very user specific and, in all honesty, not programmer friendly. Let's put the control back into the programmer's hands.

We're going to need four arguments for both the input and output files:

Since the first one is the name of the script we're creating, what we want is the name of the source file, the type of delimiter we're dealing with and the name of the destination database.

```
Dim args() As String =
System.Environment.GetCommandLineArgs()

    if len(args.Length ) < 4 then
        print ("Please enter the file you want to import, the type of delimiter used, the new table name and the destination database where you want the new table to be added.")
        WScript.Quit(-1)
    End If

    'source = args(0)
    'd = args(1)
    'tbln = args(2)
    'dest = args(3)
```

Forgetting the delimiter:

C:\Users\Administrator>C:\Users\Administrator\Desktop\args.ba
s C:\Greattimes.txt Products D:\Process.accdb
Please enter the file you want to import, the type of delimiter used, the new table name and the destination database where you want the new table to be added.

Adding the delimiter:

C:\Users\Administrator>C:\Users\Administrator\Desktop\args.ba
s C:\Greattimes.txt ~ Products D:\Process.accdb

C:\Users\Administrator\Desktop\args.bas
C:\Greattimes.txt
~

Products
D:\Process.accdb

Continuing with the code:

```
Dim args() as String =
System.Environment.GetCommandLineArgs()


  if len(args.Length ) < 4 then
    print ("Please enter the file you want to import, the type of delimiter used, the new table name and the destination database where you want the new table to be added.")
    WScript.Quit(-1)
  End If

#source = args(0)
#d = args(1)
#tbln = args(2)
#dest = args(3)

#for testing the code
source = "C:\Products.csv"
d = ","
tbln = "Products"
dest = "D:\Process.accdb"
```

```
cnstr                 =                 "Provider=MSDASQL;Extended
Properties=\"Driver={Microsoft Text Driver (*.txt; *.csv)}; hdr=yes;
format=Delimited(d); dbq=C:\\;\";"
print(cnstr)
Set rs1 = CreateObject("ADODB.Recordset")
rs1.ActiveConnection = cnstr
rs1.Cursorlocation = 3
rs1.LockType =3
rs1.Open("Select * from [Products.csv]")

Dim oAccess As Object = CreateObject("Access.Application")
oAccess.OpenCurrentDatabase("D:\Process.accdb")
Dim db As Object = oAccess.CurrentDB()
Set Dim tbldef as Object =  db.CreateTableDef(tbln)
For x = 0 To rs.fields.Count-1
   Dim fld As Object = tbldef.CreateField(rs1.Fields(x).Name, 12)
   fld.AllowZeroLength = True
   tbldef.Fields.Append(fld)
Next
db.TableDefs.Append(tbldef)

Dim rs As Object= db.OpenRecordset("Products")
Do while rs1.eof = false
   rs.AddNew()
   for x 0 to rs1.Fields.Count -1
      rs.Fields(x).Value = rs1.Fields(x).Value
   Next
   rs.Update()
   rs1.MoveNext()
 Loop
```

The result:

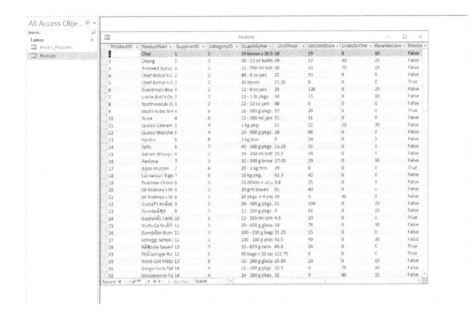

Now, let's go the other way. We want to export:

Dim args() as String = System.Environment.GetCommndLineargs()

```
#if args.length < 5 then
#    print ("Please enter the file you want to import, the type of
delimiter used, the new table name and the destination database
where you want the new table to be added.")
#    WScript.Quit(-1)
#End If

#source = args(0)
#d = args(1)
#tbln = args(2)
#dest = args(3)
```

```vb
'for testing the code
source = "D:\\Process.accdb"
d = "!"
tbln = "Process_Properties"
dest = "C:\\Process.txt"
tempstr = ""

Dim oAccess As Object = CreateObject("Access.Application")
oAccess.OpenCurrentDatabase(source)
Dim db As Object = oAccess.CurrentDB()

Dim ws As Object = CreateObject("WScript.Shell")
Dim fso As Object = CreateObject("Scripting.FileSystemObject")
Dim txtstream As Object = fso.OpenTextFile(dest, 2, True, -2)

Dim rs As Object = db.OpenRecordset(tbln)
for x = 0 to rs.Fields.Count -1
   if tempstr <> "" then
      tempstr = tempstr + d
   End If
   tempstr = tempstr + rs.Fields[x].Name
Next
txtstream.WriteLine(tempstr)
tempstr =""
Do While rs.EOF = false
   for x = 0 to rs.Fields.Count -1
      if tempstr <> "" then
         tempstr = tempstr + d
      End If
      tempstr = tempstr + chr(34) + str(rs.Fields[x].value) + chr(34)
```

```
        Next
        txtstream.WriteLine(tempstr)
        tempstr = ""
        rs.MoveNext()
Loop
txtstream.Close()
```

And the result:

```
Process - Notepad                                    —    □    ×
File  Edit  Format  View  Help
Caption!CommandLine!CreationClassName!CreationDate!CSCreationClas ^
"System Idle Process"!""!"Win32_Process"!"05/12/2018 16:58:58:07"
"System"!""!"Win32_Process"!"05/12/2018 16:58:58:07"!"Win32_Compu
"smss.exe"!""!"Win32_Process"!"05/12/2018 16:58:58:07"!"Win32_Com
"csrss.exe"!""!"Win32_Process"!"05/12/2018 16:58:58:16"!"Win32_Co
"csrss.exe"!""!"Win32_Process"!"05/12/2018 16:58:58:20"!"Win32_Co
"wininit.exe"!""!"Win32_Process"!"05/12/2018 16:58:58:20"!"Win32_
"winlogon.exe"!"winlogon.exe"!"Win32_Process"!"05/12/2018 16:58:5
"services.exe"!""!"Win32_Process"!"05/12/2018 16:58:58:24"!"Win32
"lsass.exe"!"C:\\WINDOWS\\system32\\lsass.exe"!"Win32_Process"!"0
"svchost.exe"!"C:\\WINDOWS\\system32\\svchost.exe -k DcomLaunch"!
"svchost.exe"!"C:\\WINDOWS\\system32\\svchost.exe -k RPCSS"!"Win3
"dwm.exe"!"\dwm.exe\"!"Win32_Process"!"05/12/2018 16:58:58:30"!"W
"svchost.exe"!"C:\\WINDOWS\\System32\\svchost.exe -k termsvcs"!"W
"svchost.exe"!"C:\\WINDOWS\\system32\\svchost.exe -k LocalService
"svchost.exe"!"C:\\WINDOWS\\System32\\svchost.exe -k LocalService
"svchost.exe"!"C:\\WINDOWS\\System32\\svchost.exe -k LocalSystemN
"svchost.exe"!"C:\\WINDOWS\\system32\\svchost.exe -k NetworkServi
"svchost.exe"!"C:\\WINDOWS\\system32\\svchost.exe -k LocalService
"NVDisplay.Container.exe"!"\C:\\Program Files\\NVIDIA Corporation
"svchost.exe"!"C:\\WINDOWS\\system32\\svchost.exe -k netsvcs"!"Wi
"WUDFHost.exe"!"\C:\\Windows\\System32\\WUDFHost.exe\ -HostGUID:1
380"!"0"!"0"
"svchost.exe"!"C:\\WINDOWS\\system32\\svchost.exe -k LocalService
"svchost.exe"!"C:\\WINDOWS\\system32\\svchost.exe -k NetworkServi
"svchost.exe"!"C:\\WINDOWS\\System32\\svchost.exe -k LocalService
"svchost.exe"!"C:\\WINDOWS\\System32\\svchost.exe -k smbsvcs"!"Wi
"spoolsv.exe"!"C:\\WINDOWS\\System32\\spoolsv.exe"!"Win32_Process
"svchost.exe"!"C:\\WINDOWS\\system32\\svchost.exe -k apphost"!"Wi
<                                                                >
```

So, now, we have two totally customized VB.NET scripts which enable importing and exporting files to Access. The rest of our export functions will be based on connecting to Access and enumerating through what we've created

ROUTINES WE ARE WRITNG FOR ACCESS

The routines being used in the book

Creating forms, writing code in VB.NET is not something you want to do if you are a VB.NET programmer. I know I wouldn't. So, with that in mind, this book is staying out of the internal workings of what Access does and connecting to Access to connect or create databases, create and populate tables and establish connections with recordsets we want to use to display information. We will be creating:

- ASP
- ASPX
- Attribute XML
- Colon Delimited Text Files
- Comma Delimited Text Files
- Element XML
- Element XML For XSL
- Exclamation Delimited Text Files
- Excel Automation
- Excel Spreadsheet

- Excel using a CSV File
- HTA
- HTML
- Schema XML
- Semi Colon Delimited File
- Tab Delimited File
- Tilde Delimited File
- XSL Files

With that said, it is time to look at the way this e-book uses Access and after that, we will start building code from those routines.

THE SOURCE CODE

Programming for effect

You can't write code without knowing the building blocks
needed to write it.
—R. T. Edwards

T here is nothing more important than knowing what the code is doing to get the job done. How can you fix an issue with it if you can't find the issue? One of the reasons why I was good at solving customers' issues was because I was able to look at the code and could spot the problem.

With that thought freshly in your mind, since we are dealing with a Database and a recordset, we can use the field names for our headers and the field values for our data.

But we start with this first:

```
Dim oAccess As Object = CreateObject("Access.Application")
oAccess.OpenCurrentDatabase(DBName)
Dim db As Object =oAccess.CurrentDB()
```

```
Dim rs As Object = db.OpenRecordset(TBLName)
```

At this point, we shouldn't have to write this continually. However, because we are writing code as separate entities, you will need to add the above code in each one.

ASP CODE

T

HERE IS NOTING FANTASIC ABOUT CREATING ASP OR ASPX WEB PAGES. In fact, additional hoops must be jumped - web site where you can cut and paste what you just created from here is one of them. So, with that said, I've added enough bells and whistles into the code structure to make it worth your while. Here's what is in store for you:

- Report View
  - Horizontal
    - None
    - Button
    - Combobox
    - Div
    - Link
    - Listbox
    - Span

- - - Textarea
    - Textbox
  - Vertical
    - None
    - Button
    - Combobox
    - Div
    - Link
    - Listbox
    - Span
    - Textarea
    - Textbox

- Table View
  - Horizontal
    - None
    - Button
    - Combobox
    - Div
    - Link
    - Listbox
    - Span
    - Textarea
    - Textbox
  - Vertical
    - None
    - Button
    - Combobox
    - Div
    - Link
    - Listbox
    - Span
    - Textarea

- Textbox

```
Dim ws As Object = CreateObject("WScript.Shell")
Dim fso As Object = CreateObject("Scripting.FileSystemObject")
Dim txtstream As Object =fso.OpenTextFile(ws.CurrentDirectory +
"\Products.asp", 2, true, -2)
txtstream.WriteLine("<html>")
txtstream.WriteLine("<head>")
txtstream.WriteLine("<title>" + Tablename + "</title>")
#Add Stylesheet here
txtstream.WriteLine("<body>")
txtstream.WriteLine("</br>")
```

Horizontal Reports

```
txtstream.WriteLine("<table border=0 cellspacing=3 cellpadding=3>")
txtstream.WriteLine("<%")
txtstream.WriteLine("Response.Write("""<tr>""" + vbcrlf)")
For x = 0 to rs.Fields.Count-1
    txtstream.WriteLine("Response.Write("""<th    style=""    font-family:Calibri,
Sans-Serif;font-size:  12px;color:darkred;"""   align='left'  nowrap='nowrap'>"  +
rs.Fields(x).Name + "</th>""" + vbcrlf)")
Next
txtstream.WriteLine("Response.Write("""</tr>""" + vbcrlf)")
Do While(rs.EOF = false)
    txtstream.WriteLine("Response.Write("""<tr>""" + vbcrlf)")
    For x = 0 to rs.Fields.Count-1
```

NONE

```
        txtstream.WriteLine("Response.Write("""<td   style="""font-family:Calibri,
Sans-Serif;font-size:  12px;color:navy;"""   align='left'   nowrap='nowrap'>"   +
rs.Fields(x).Value + "</td>""" + vbcrlf)")
```

Button

```
txtstream.WriteLine("Response.Write("""<td   style="""font-family:Calibri,
Sans-Serif;font-size:   12px;color:navy;"""   align='left'   nowrap='true'><button
style='width:100%;' value ='" + rs.Fields(x).Value + "'>" + rs.Fields(x).Value +
"</button></td>""" + vbcrlf)")
```

COMBOBOX

```
txtstream.WriteLine("Response.Write("""<td   style="""font-family:Calibri,
Sans-Serif;font-size: 12px;color:navy;""" align='left' nowrap='true'><select><option
value   =   """"   +   rs.Fields(x).Value   +   """">"   +   rs.Fields(x).Value   +
"</option></select></td>""" + vbcrlf)")
```

DIV

```
txtstream.WriteLine("Response.Write("""<td   style="""font-family:Calibri,
Sans-Serif;font-size:   12px;color:navy;"""   align='left'   nowrap='true'><div>"   +
rs.Fields(x).Value + "</div></td>""" + vbcrlf)")
```

LINK

```
txtstream.WriteLine("Response.Write("""<td   style="""font-family:Calibri,
Sans-Serif;font-size: 12px;color:navy;""" align='left' nowrap='true'><a href='"   +
rs.Fields(x).Value + "'>" + rs.Fields(x).Value + "</a></td>""" + vbcrlf)")
```

LISTBOX

```
txtstream.WriteLine("Response.Write("""<td   style="""font-family:Calibri,
Sans-Serif;font-size:   12px;color:navy;"""   align='left'   nowrap='true'><select
multiple><option value = """" + rs.Fields(x).Value + """">" + rs.Fields(x).Value +
"</option></select></td>""" + vbcrlf)")
```

SPAN

```
txtstream.WriteLine("Response.Write("""<td   style="""font-family:Calibri,
Sans-Serif;font-size:   12px;color:navy;"""   align='left'   nowrap='true'><span>"   +
rs.Fields(x).Value + "</span></td>""" + vbcrlf)")
```

TEXTAREA

```
        txtstream.WriteLine("Response.Write(""""<td   style=""""font-family:Calibri,
Sans-Serif;font-size: 12px;color:navy;"""" align='left' nowrap='true'><textarea>" +
rs.Fields(x).Value + "</textarea></td>"""" + vbcrlf)")
```

TEXTBOX

```
        txtstream.WriteLine("Response.Write(""""<td   style=""""font-family:Calibri,
Sans-Serif;font-size:   12px;color:navy;""""   align='left'   nowrap='true'><input
type=text value=""""" + rs.Fields(x).Value + """"""></input></td>"""" + vbcrlf)")
        Next
        txtstream.WriteLine("Response.Write(""""</tr>"""" + vbcrlf)")
        rs.MoveNext
Loop
txtstream.WriteLine("%>")
txtstream.WriteLine("</table>")
txtstream.WriteLine("</body>")
txtstream.WriteLine("</html>")
txtstream.Close()
```

Vertical Reports

```
txtstream.WriteLine("<table border=0 cellspacing=3 cellpadding=3>")
txtstream.WriteLine("<%")
For x = 0 to rs.Fields.Count-1
        txtstream.WriteLine("Response.Write(""""<tr><th        style=""""      font-
family:Calibri,     Sans-Serif;font-size:     12px;color:darkred;""""     align='left'
nowrap='nowrap'>" + rs.Fields(x).Name + "</th>"""" + vbcrlf)")
        rs.MoveFirst()
        Do While(rs.EOF = false)
        txtstream.WriteLine("Response.Write(""""<td    style=""""font-family:Calibri,
Sans-Serif;font-size: 12px;color:navy;"""">" + rs.Fields(x).Value + "</td>"""" +
vbcrlf)")
```

NONE

```
        txtstream.WriteLine("Response.Write(""""<td   style=""""font-family:Calibri,
Sans-Serif;font-size:   12px;color:navy;""""   align='left'   nowrap='nowrap'>"   +
rs.Fields(x).Value + "</td>"""" + vbcrlf)")
```

Button

```
        txtstream.WriteLine("Response.Write(""""<td    style=""""font-family:Calibri,
Sans-Serif;font-size:   12px;color:navy;""""    align='left'   nowrap='true'><button
style='width:100%;' value ='" + rs.Fields(x).Value + "'>" + rs.Fields(x).Value +
"</button></td>"""" + vbcrlf)")
```

Combobox

```
        txtstream.WriteLine("Response.Write(""""<td    style=""""font-family:Calibri,
Sans-Serif;font-size: 12px;color:navy;"""" align='left' nowrap='true'><select><option
value    =    """"    +    rs.Fields(x).Value    +    """">"    +    rs.Fields(x).Value    +
"</option></select></td>"""" + vbcrlf)")
```

Div

```
        txtstream.WriteLine("Response.Write(""""<td    style=""""font-family:Calibri,
Sans-Serif;font-size:   12px;color:navy;""""    align='left'   nowrap='true'><div>"   +
rs.Fields(x).Value + "</div></td>"""" + vbcrlf)")
```

Link

```
        txtstream.WriteLine("Response.Write(""""<td style=""""font-family:Calibri, Sans-
Serif;font-size:  12px;color:navy;""""   align='left'   nowrap='true'><a   href='"   +
rs.Fields(x).Value + "'>" + rs.Fields(x).Value + "</a></td>"""" + vbcrlf)")
```

Listbox

```
        txtstream.WriteLine("Response.Write(""""<td style=""""font-family:Calibri, Sans-
Serif;font-size:    12px;color:navy;""""    align='left'    nowrap='true'><select
multiple><option value = """" + rs.Fields(x).Value + """">" + rs.Fields(x).Value +
"</option></select></td>"""" + vbcrlf)")
```

Span

```
        txtstream.WriteLine("Response.Write(""<td      style="""font-family:Calibri,
Sans-Serif;font-size: 12px;color:navy;""" align='left' nowrap='true'><span>" +
rs.Fields(x).Value + "</span></td>""" + vbcrlf)")
```

Textarea

```
    txtstream.WriteLine("Response.Write(""<td style="""font-family:Calibri, Sans-
Serif;font-size:  12px;color:navy;"""  align='left'  nowrap='true'><textarea>"  +
rs.Fields(x).Value + "</textarea></td>""" + vbcrlf)")
```

Textbox

```
        txtstream.WriteLine("Response.Write(""<td      style="""font-family:Calibri,
Sans-Serif;font-size:    12px;color:navy;"""    align='left'    nowrap='true'><input
type=text value=""" + rs.Fields(x).Value + """"></input></td>""" + vbcrlf)")
        rs.MoveNext
    loop
    txtstream.WriteLine("Response.Write(""</tr>""" + vbcrlf)")
Next
txtstream.WriteLine("%>")
txtstream.WriteLine("</table>")
txtstream.WriteLine("</body>")
txtstream.WriteLine("</html>")
txtstream.Close()
```

Horizontal Tables

```
    txtstream.WriteLine("<table        style='border:Double;border-width:1px;border-
color:navy;' rules=all frames=both cellpadding=2 cellspacing=2 Width=0>")
    txtstream.WriteLine("<%")
    txtstream.WriteLine("Response.Write(""<tr>""" + vbcrlf)")
    For x = 0 to rs.Fields.Count-1
    txtstream.WriteLine("Response.Write(""<th      style="""  font-family:Calibri,
Sans-Serif;font-size: 12px;color:darkred;""" align='left' nowrap='nowrap'>" +
rs.Fields(x).Name + "</th>""" + vbcrlf)")

    Next
```

```
txtstream.WriteLine("Response.Write(""</tr>""" + vbcrlf)")
Do While(rs.EOF = false)
  txtstream.WriteLine("Response.Write(""<tr>""" + vbcrlf)")
    For x = 0 to rs.Fields.Count-1
```

NONE

```
        txtstream.WriteLine("Response.Write(""<td   style=""font-family:Calibri,
Sans-Serif;font-size:   12px;color:navy;""   align='left'   nowrap='nowrap'>"   +
rs.Fields(x).Value + "</td>""" + vbcrlf)")
```

Button

```
        txtstream.WriteLine("Response.Write(""<td   style=""font-family:Calibri,
Sans-Serif;font-size:   12px;color:navy;""   align='left'   nowrap='true'><button
style='width:100%;' value ="' + rs.Fields(x).Value + "'>" + rs.Fields(x).Value +
"</button></td>""" + vbcrlf)")
```

COMBOBOX

```
        txtstream.WriteLine("Response.Write(""<td   style=""font-family:Calibri,
Sans-Serif;font-size: 12px;color:navy;"" align='left' nowrap='true'><select><option
value  =   """   +   rs.Fields(x).Value   +   """>"   +   rs.Fields(x).Value   +
"</option></select></td>""" + vbcrlf)")
```

DIV

```
        txtstream.WriteLine("Response.Write(""<td   style=""font-family:Calibri,
Sans-Serif;font-size:   12px;color:navy;""   align='left'   nowrap='true'><div>"   +
rs.Fields(x).Value + "</div></td>""" + vbcrlf)")
```

LINK

```
        txtstream.WriteLine("Response.Write(""<td   style=""font-family:Calibri,
Sans-Serif;font-size: 12px;color:navy;"" align='left' nowrap='true'><a href='" +
rs.Fields(x).Value + "'>" + rs.Fields(x).Value + "</a></td>""" + vbcrlf)")
```

LISTBOX

```
        txtstream.WriteLine("Response.Write(""""<td   style=""""font-family:Calibri,
Sans-Serif;font-size:   12px;color:navy;""""   align='left'   nowrap='true'><select
multiple><option value = """""" + rs.Fields(x).Value + """""">" + rs.Fields(x).Value +
"</option></select></td>"""" + vbcrlf)")
```

SPAN

```
        txtstream.WriteLine("Response.Write(""""<td   style=""""font-family:Calibri,
Sans-Serif;font-size:  12px;color:navy;""""   align='left'   nowrap='true'><span>"   +
rs.Fields(x).Value + "</span></td>"""" + vbcrlf)")
```

TEXTAREA

```
        txtstream.WriteLine("Response.Write(""""<td   style=""""font-family:Calibri,
Sans-Serif;font-size: 12px;color:navy;""""  align='left'  nowrap='true'><textarea>"  +
rs.Fields(x).Value + "</textarea></td>"""" + vbcrlf)")
```

TEXTBOX

```
        txtstream.WriteLine("Response.Write(""""<td   style=""""font-family:Calibri,
Sans-Serif;font-size:   12px;color:navy;""""   align='left'   nowrap='true'><input
type=text value="""""" + rs.Fields(x).Value + """"""></input></td>"""" + vbcrlf)")

    txtstream.WriteLine("Response.Write(""""</tr>"""" + vbcrlf)")
    rs.MoveNext

txtstream.WriteLine("%>")
txtstream.WriteLine("</table>")
txtstream.WriteLine("</body>")
txtstream.WriteLine("</html>")
txtstream.Close()
```

Vertical Tables

```
    txtstream.WriteLine("<table        style='border:Double;border-width:1px;border-
color:navy;' rules=all frames=both cellpadding=2 cellspacing=2 Width=0>")
```

```
txtstream.WriteLine("<%")

For x = 0 to rs.Fields.Count-1
    txtstream.WriteLine("Response.Write(""<tr><th        style=""    font-
family:Calibri,    Sans-Serif;font-size:    12px;color:darkred;""    align='left'
nowrap='nowrap'>" + rs.Fields(x).Name + "</th>""" + vbcrlf)")
    rs.MoveFirst()
    Do While(rs.EOF = false)
    txtstream.WriteLine("Response.Write(""<td    style=""font-family:Calibri,
Sans-Serif;font-size:  12px;color:navy;"">" + rs.Fields(x).Value + "</td>"""  +
vbcrlf)")
```

NONE

```
    txtstream.WriteLine("Response.Write(""<td  style=""font-family:Calibri,
Sans-Serif;font-size:  12px;color:navy;""   align='left'   nowrap='nowrap'>"  +
rs.Fields(x).Value + "</td>""" + vbcrlf)")
```

Button

```
    txtstream.WriteLine("Response.Write(""<td    style=""font-family:Calibri,
Sans-Serif;font-size:  12px;color:navy;""   align='left'   nowrap='true'><button
style='width:100%;' value ='" + rs.Fields(x).Value + "'>" + rs.Fields(x).Value +
"</button></td>""" + vbcrlf)")
```

Combobox

```
    txtstream.WriteLine("Response.Write(""<td    style=""font-family:Calibri,
Sans-Serif;font-size: 12px;color:navy;"" align='left' nowrap='true'><select><option
value  =  """   +   rs.Fields(x).Value   +   """>"   +   rs.Fields(x).Value   +
"</option></select></td>""" + vbcrlf)")
```

Div

```
    txtstream.WriteLine("Response.Write(""<td       style=""font-family:Calibri,
Sans-Serif;font-size:  12px;color:navy;""   align='left'   nowrap='true'><div>"  +
rs.Fields(x).Value + "</div></td>""" + vbcrlf)")
```

Link

```
txtstream.WriteLine("Response.Write(""<td style="""font-family:Calibri, Sans-Serif;font-size: 12px;color:navy;""" align='left' nowrap='true'><a href='" + rs.Fields(x).Value + "'>" + rs.Fields(x).Value + "</a></td>""" + vbcrlf)")
```

Listbox

```
txtstream.WriteLine("Response.Write(""<td style="""font-family:Calibri, Sans-Serif;font-size: 12px;color:navy;""" align='left' nowrap='true'><select multiple><option value = """ + rs.Fields(x).Value + """>" + rs.Fields(x).Value + "</option></select></td>""" + vbcrlf)")
```

Span

```
txtstream.WriteLine("Response.Write(""<td style="""font-family:Calibri, Sans-Serif;font-size: 12px;color:navy;""" align='left' nowrap='true'><span>" + rs.Fields(x).Value + "</span></td>""" + vbcrlf)")
```

Textarea

```
txtstream.WriteLine("Response.Write(""<td style="""font-family:Calibri, Sans-Serif;font-size: 12px;color:navy;""" align='left' nowrap='true'><textarea>" + rs.Fields(x).Value + "</textarea></td>""" + vbcrlf)")
```

Textbox

```
txtstream.WriteLine("Response.Write(""<td style="""font-family:Calibri, Sans-Serif;font-size: 12px;color:navy;""" align='left' nowrap='true'><input type=text value="""" + rs.Fields(x).Value + """"></input></td>""" + vbcrlf)")
        rs.MoveNext

    txtstream.WriteLine("Response.Write(""</tr>""" + vbcrlf)")

txtstream.WriteLine("%>")
txtstream.WriteLine("</table>")
txtstream.WriteLine("</body>")
```

```
txtstream.WriteLine("</html>")
txtstream.Close()
```

ASPX CODE

ELOW ARE EXAMPLES OF USING ADO THROUGH VBSCRIPT TO CREATE ASPX FILES.

```
Dim ws As Object = CreateObject("WScript.Shell")
Dim fso As Object = CreateObject("Scripting.FileSystemObject")
Dim txtstream As Object =fso.OpenTextFile(ws.CurrentDirectory +
"\Products.asp", 2, true, -2)
txtstream.WriteLine("<html>")
txtstream.WriteLine("<head>")
txtstream.WriteLine("<title>" + Tablename + "</title>")
#Add Stylesheet here
txtstream.WriteLine("<body>")
txtstream.WriteLine("</br>")
```

Horizontal Reports

```
txtstream.WriteLine("<table border=0 cellspacing=3 cellpadding=3>")
txtstream.WriteLine("<%")
txtstream.WriteLine("Response.Write(""<tr>""" + vbcrlf)")
For x = 0 to rs.Fields.Count-1
```

txtstream.WriteLine("Response.Write(""""<th style="""" font-family:Calibri, Sans-Serif;font-size: 12px;color:darkred;"""" align='left' nowrap='nowrap'>" + rs.Fields(x).Name + "</th>"""" + vbcrlf)")
    Next
txtstream.WriteLine("Response.Write(""""</tr>"""" + vbcrlf)")
    Do While(rs.EOF = false)
        txtstream.WriteLine("Response.Write(""""<tr>"""" + vbcrlf)")
        For x = 0 to rs.Fields.Count-1

NONE

txtstream.WriteLine("Response.Write(""""<td style="""""font-family:Calibri, Sans-Serif;font-size: 12px;color:navy;"""" align='left' nowrap='nowrap'>" + rs.Fields(x).Value + "</td>"""" + vbcrlf)")

Button

txtstream.WriteLine("Response.Write(""""<td style="""""font-family:Calibri, Sans-Serif;font-size: 12px;color:navy;"""" align='left' nowrap='true'><button style='width:100%;' value ='" + rs.Fields(x).Value + "'>" + rs.Fields(x).Value + "</button></td>"""" + vbcrlf)")

COMBOBOX

txtstream.WriteLine("Response.Write(""""<td style="""""font-family:Calibri, Sans-Serif;font-size: 12px;color:navy;"""" align='left' nowrap='true'><select><option value = """"" + rs.Fields(x).Value + """"">" + rs.Fields(x).Value + "</option></select></td>"""" + vbcrlf)")

DIV

txtstream.WriteLine("Response.Write(""""<td style="""""font-family:Calibri, Sans-Serif;font-size: 12px;color:navy;"""" align='left' nowrap='true'> " + rs.Fields(x).Value + " </td>"""" + vbcrlf)")

LINK

```
        txtstream.WriteLine("Response.Write("""<td    style="""font-family:Calibri,
Sans-Serif;font-size: 12px;color:navy;""" align='left' nowrap='true'><a href='" +
rs.Fields(x).Value + "'>" + rs.Fields(x).Value + "</a></td>""" + vbcrlf)")
```

LISTBOX

```
        txtstream.WriteLine("Response.Write("""<td    style="""font-family:Calibri,
Sans-Serif;font-size:  12px;color:navy;"""   align='left'   nowrap='true'><select
multiple><option value = """ + rs.Fields(x).Value + """">" + rs.Fields(x).Value +
"</option></select></td>""" + vbcrlf)")
```

SPAN

```
        txtstream.WriteLine("Response.Write("""<td    style="""font-family:Calibri,
Sans-Serif;font-size:  12px;color:navy;"""  align='left'  nowrap='true'><span>"  +
rs.Fields(x).Value + "</span></td>""" + vbcrlf)")
```

TEXTAREA

```
        txtstream.WriteLine("Response.Write("""<td    style="""font-family:Calibri,
Sans-Serif;font-size: 12px;color:navy;""" align='left' nowrap='true'><textarea>" +
rs.Fields(x).Value + "</textarea></td>""" + vbcrlf)")
```

TEXTBOX

```
        txtstream.WriteLine("Response.Write("""<td    style="""font-family:Calibri,
Sans-Serif;font-size:   12px;color:navy;"""   align='left'   nowrap='true'><input
type=text value="""" + rs.Fields(x).Value + """"></input></td>""" + vbcrlf)")

    Next
    txtstream.WriteLine("Response.Write("""</tr>""" + vbcrlf)")
    rs.MoveNext
Loop
txtstream.WriteLine("%>")
txtstream.WriteLine("</table>")
txtstream.WriteLine("</body>")
txtstream.WriteLine("</html>")
txtstream.Close()
```

Vertical Reports

```
txtstream.WriteLine("<table border=0 cellspacing=3 cellpadding=3>")
txtstream.WriteLine("<%")
For x = 0 to rs.Fields.Count-1
        txtstream.WriteLine("Response.Write(""<tr><th        style=""        font-
family:Calibri,        Sans-Serif;font-size:        12px;color:darkred;""        align='left'
nowrap='nowrap'>" + rs.Fields(x).Name + "</th>""" + vbcrlf)")
        rs.MoveFirst()
        Do While(rs.EOF = false)
        txtstream.WriteLine("Response.Write(""<td    style=""font-family:Calibri,
Sans-Serif;font-size: 12px;color:navy;"">"  +  rs.Fields(x).Value  +  "</td>"""  +
vbcrlf)")
```

NONE

```
        txtstream.WriteLine("Response.Write(""<td  style=""font-family:Calibri,
Sans-Serif;font-size:    12px;color:navy;""    align='left'    nowrap='nowrap'>"    +
rs.Fields(x).Value + "</td>""" + vbcrlf)")
```

Button

```
        txtstream.WriteLine("Response.Write(""<td    style=""font-family:Calibri,
Sans-Serif;font-size:   12px;color:navy;""   align='left'   nowrap='true'><button
style='width:100%;' value ="" + rs.Fields(x).Value + "'>" + rs.Fields(x).Value +
"</button></td>""" + vbcrlf)")
```

Combobox

```
        txtstream.WriteLine("Response.Write(""<td    style=""font-family:Calibri,
Sans-Serif;font-size: 12px;color:navy;"" align='left' nowrap='true'><select><option
value   =   """   +   rs.Fields(x).Value   +   """>"   +   rs.Fields(x).Value   +
"</option></select></td>""" + vbcrlf)")
```

Div

```
txtstream.WriteLine("Response.Write("""<td        style="""font-family:Calibri,
Sans-Serif;font-size:  12px;color:navy;"""  align='left'  nowrap='true'><div>"  +
rs.Fields(x).Value + "</div></td>""" + vbcrlf)")
```

Link

```
txtstream.WriteLine("Response.Write("""<td style="""font-family:Calibri, Sans-
Serif;font-size:  12px;color:navy;"""  align='left'  nowrap='true'><a  href='"  +
rs.Fields(x).Value + "'>" + rs.Fields(x).Value + "</a></td>""" + vbcrlf)")
```

Listbox

```
txtstream.WriteLine("Response.Write("""<td style="""font-family:Calibri, Sans-
Serif;font-size:     12px;color:navy;"""     align='left'     nowrap='true'><select
multiple><option value = """ + rs.Fields(x).Value + """">" + rs.Fields(x).Value +
"</option></select></td>""" + vbcrlf)")
```

Span

```
txtstream.WriteLine("Response.Write("""<td       style="""font-family:Calibri,
Sans-Serif;font-size: 12px;color:navy;""" align='left' nowrap='true'><span>" +
rs.Fields(x).Value + "</span></td>""" + vbcrlf)")
```

Textarea

```
txtstream.WriteLine("Response.Write("""<td style="""font-family:Calibri, Sans-
Serif;font-size:  12px;color:navy;"""  align='left'  nowrap='true'><textarea>"  +
rs.Fields(x).Value + "</textarea></td>""" + vbcrlf)")
```

Textbox

```
txtstream.WriteLine("Response.Write("""<td       style="""font-family:Calibri,
Sans-Serif;font-size:   12px;color:navy;"""   align='left'   nowrap='true'><input
type=text value="""" + rs.Fields(x).Value + """"></input></td>""" + vbcrlf)")
        rs.MoveNext
        Loop
        txtstream.WriteLine("Response.Write("""</tr>""" + vbcrlf)")
```

```
Next
txtstream.WriteLine("%>")
txtstream.WriteLine("</table>")
txtstream.WriteLine("</body>")
txtstream.WriteLine("</html>")
txtstream.Close()
```

Horizontal Tables

```
txtstream.WriteLine("<table          style='border:Double;border-width:1px;border-
color:navy;' rules=all frames=both cellpadding=2 cellspacing=2 Width=0>")
txtstream.WriteLine("<%")
txtstream.WriteLine("Response.Write(""<tr>""" + vbcrlf)")
For x = 0 to rs.Fields.Count-1
    txtstream.WriteLine("Response.Write(""<th    style=""    font-family:Calibri,
Sans-Serif;font-size:  12px;color:darkred;""  align='left'  nowrap='nowrap'>" +
rs.Fields(x).Name + "</th>""" + vbcrlf)")
Next
txtstream.WriteLine("Response.Write(""</tr>""" + vbcrlf)")
Do While(rs.EOF = false)
   txtstream.WriteLine("Response.Write(""<tr>""" + vbcrlf)")
      For x = 0 to rs.Fields.Count-1
```

NONE

```
        txtstream.WriteLine("Response.Write(""<td  style=""font-family:Calibri,
Sans-Serif;font-size:  12px;color:navy;""  align='left'  nowrap='nowrap'>" +
rs.Fields(x).Value + "</td>""" + vbcrlf)")
```

Button

```
        txtstream.WriteLine("Response.Write(""<td  style=""font-family:Calibri,
Sans-Serif;font-size:  12px;color:navy;""  align='left'  nowrap='true'><button
style='width:100%;' value ='" + rs.Fields(x).Value + "'>" + rs.Fields(x).Value +
"</button></td>""" + vbcrlf)")
```

COMBOBOX

```
        txtstream.WriteLine("Response.Write("""<td   style="""font-family:Calibri,
Sans-Serif;font-size: 12px;color:navy;""" align='left' nowrap='true'><select><option
value   =   """   +   rs.Fields(x).Value   +   """">"   +   rs.Fields(x).Value   +
"</option></select></td>""" + vbcrlf)")
```

DIV

```
        txtstream.WriteLine("Response.Write("""<td   style="""font-family:Calibri,
Sans-Serif;font-size:  12px;color:navy;"""  align='left'  nowrap='true'><div>"   +
rs.Fields(x).Value + "</div></td>""" + vbcrlf)")
```

LINK

```
        txtstream.WriteLine("Response.Write("""<td   style="""font-family:Calibri,
Sans-Serif;font-size: 12px;color:navy;""" align='left' nowrap='true'><a href='" +
rs.Fields(x).Value + "'>" + rs.Fields(x).Value + "</a></td>""" + vbcrlf)")
```

LISTBOX

```
        txtstream.WriteLine("Response.Write("""<td   style="""font-family:Calibri,
Sans-Serif;font-size:    12px;color:navy;"""    align='left'    nowrap='true'><select
multiple><option value = """ + rs.Fields(x).Value + """">" + rs.Fields(x).Value +
"</option></select></td>""" + vbcrlf)")
```

SPAN

```
        txtstream.WriteLine("Response.Write("""<td   style="""font-family:Calibri,
Sans-Serif;font-size: 12px;color:navy;""" align='left' nowrap='true'><span>"   +
rs.Fields(x).Value + "</span></td>""" + vbcrlf)")
```

TEXTAREA

```
        txtstream.WriteLine("Response.Write("""<td   style="""font-family:Calibri,
Sans-Serif;font-size: 12px;color:navy;""" align='left' nowrap='true'><textarea>"   +
rs.Fields(x).Value + "</textarea></td>""" + vbcrlf)")
```

TEXTBOX

```
        txtstream.WriteLine("Response.Write(""<td   style=""font-family:Calibri,
Sans-Serif;font-size:   12px;color:navy;""    align='left'   nowrap='true'><input
type=text value=""" + rs.Fields(x).Value + """></input></td>"" + vbcrlf)")
        Next
        txtstream.WriteLine("Response.Write(""</tr>"" + vbcrlf)")
        rs.MoveNext
    Loop
    txtstream.WriteLine("%>")
    txtstream.WriteLine("</table>")
    txtstream.WriteLine("</body>")
    txtstream.WritcLinc("</html>")
    txtstream.Close()
```

Vertical Tables

```
    txtstream.WriteLine("<table       style='border:Double;border-width:1px;border-
color:navy;' rules=all frames=both cellpadding=2 cellspacing=2 Width=0>")
    txtstream.WriteLine("<%")
    For x = 0 to rs.Fields.Count-1
        txtstream.WriteLine("Response.Write(""<tr><th       style=""    font-
family:Calibri,   Sans-Serif;font-size:   12px;color:darkred;""    align='left'
nowrap='nowrap'>" + rs.Fields(x).Name + "</th>"" + vbcrlf)")
        rs.MoveFirst()
        Do While rs.EOF = false
        txtstream.WriteLine("Response.Write(""<td   style=""font-family:Calibri,
Sans-Serif;font-size:  12px;color:navy;"">"  +  rs.Fields(x).Value  +  "</td>""  +
vbcrlf)")
```

NONE

```
        txtstream.WriteLine("Response.Write(""<td  style=""font-family:Calibri,
Sans-Serif;font-size:   12px;color:navy;""    align='left'   nowrap='nowrap'>"   +
rs.Fields(x).Value + "</td>"" + vbcrlf)")
```

Button

```
        txtstream.WriteLine("Response.Write("""<td    style="""font-family:Calibri,
Sans-Serif;font-size:  12px;color:navy;"""  align='left'  nowrap='true'><button
style='width:100%;' value ='" + rs.Fields(x).Value + "'>" + rs.Fields(x).Value +
"</button></td>""" + vbcrlf)")
```

Combobox

```
        txtstream.WriteLine("Response.Write("""<td    style="""font-family:Calibri,
Sans-Serif;font-size: 12px;color:navy;""" align='left' nowrap='true'><select><option
value   =   """   +   rs.Fields(x).Value   +   """">"   +   rs.Fields(x).Value   +
"</option></select></td>""" + vbcrlf)")
```

Div

```
        txtstream.WriteLine("Response.Write("""<td    style="""font-family:Calibri,
Sans-Serif;font-size:  12px;color:navy;"""  align='left'  nowrap='true'><div>"  +
rs.Fields(x).Value + "</div></td>""" + vbcrlf)")
```

Link

```
        txtstream.WriteLine("Response.Write("""<td style="""font-family:Calibri, Sans-
Serif;font-size:  12px;color:navy;"""  align='left'  nowrap='true'><a  href='"  +
rs.Fields(x).Value + "'>" + rs.Fields(x).Value + "</a></td>""" + vbcrlf)")
```

Listbox

```
        txtstream.WriteLine("Response.Write("""<td style="""font-family:Calibri, Sans-
Serif;font-size:   12px;color:navy;"""   align='left'   nowrap='true'><select
multiple><option value = """ + rs.Fields(x).Value + """">" + rs.Fields(x).Value +
"</option></select></td>""" + vbcrlf)")
```

Span

```
        txtstream.WriteLine("Response.Write("""<td    style="""font-family:Calibri,
Sans-Serif;font-size: 12px;color:navy;""" align='left' nowrap='true'><span>" +
rs.Fields(x).Value + "</span></td>""" + vbcrlf)")
```

Textarea

txtstream.WriteLine("Response.Write("""<td style="""font-family:Calibri, Sans-Serif;font-size: 12px;color:navy;""" align='left' nowrap='true'><textarea>" + rs.Fields(x).Value + "</textarea></td>""" + vbcrlf)")

Textbox

txtstream.WriteLine("Response.Write("""<td style="""font-family:Calibri, Sans-Serif;font-size: 12px;color:navy;""" align='left' nowrap='true'><input type=text value="""" + rs.Fields(x).Value + """"></input></td>""" + vbcrlf)")
   rs.MoveNext
   loop
   txtstream.WriteLine("Response.Write("""</tr>""" + vbcrlf)")
  next
txtstream.WriteLine("%>")
txtstream.WriteLine("</table>")
txtstream.WriteLine("</body>")
txtstream.WriteLine("</html>")
txtstream.Close()

HTA CODE

L

IKE ASP AND ASPX, HTA BEEN AROUND FOR SOME TIME NOW. Despite the fact the concept appears to be old or outdated You should know that it is still being used as HTML as an EXE.

```
Dim ws As Object =  CreateObject("WScript.Shell")
Dim fso As Object =  CreateObject("Scripting.FileSystemObject")
Dim   txtstream   As   Object   =fso.OpenTextFile(ws.CurrentDirectory   +
"\Products.hta", 2, true, -2)
txtstream.WriteLine("<html>")
txtstream.WriteLine("<head>")
txtstream.WriteLine("<HTA:APPLICATION ")
txtstream.WriteLine("ID = ""Products"" ")
txtstream.WriteLine("APPLICATIONNAME = ""Products"" ")
txtstream.WriteLine("SCROLL = ""yes"" ")
txtstream.WriteLine("SINGLEINSTANCE = ""yes"" ")
txtstream.WriteLine("WINDOWSTATE = ""maximize"" >")
txtstream.WriteLine("<title>" + Tablename + "</title>")
#Add Stylesheet here
txtstream.WriteLine("<body>")
txtstream.WriteLine("</br>")
```

```
txtstream.WriteLine("<table border=0 cellspacing=3 cellpadding=3>")
txtstream.WriteLine("<tr>")
For x = 0 to rs.Fields.Count-1
    txtstream.WriteLine("<th style="" font-family:Calibri, Sans-Serif;font-size:
12px;color:darkred;"" align='left' nowrap='nowrap'>" + rs.Fields(x).Name +
"</th>")
Next
txtstream.WriteLine("</tr>")
Do While(rs.EOF = false)
    txtstream.WriteLine("<tr>")
    For x = 0 to rs.Fields.Count-1
```

NONE

```
        txtstream.WriteLine("<td style="""font-family:Calibri, Sans-Serif;font-
size: 12px;color:navy;"" align='left' nowrap='nowrap'>" + rs.Fields(x).Value +
"</td>")
```

Button

```
        txtstream.WriteLine("<td style="""font-family:Calibri, Sans-Serif;font-
size: 12px;color:navy;"" align='left' nowrap='true'><button style='width:100%;'
value ='" + rs.Fields(x).Value + "'>" + rs.Fields(x).Value + "</button></td>")
```

COMBOBOX

```
        txtstream.WriteLine("<td style="""font-family:Calibri, Sans-Serif;font-
size: 12px;color:navy;"" align='left' nowrap='true'><select><option value = """ +
rs.Fields(x).Value + """>" + rs.Fields(x).Value + "</option></select></td>")
```

DIV

```
        txtstream.WriteLine("<td style="""font-family:Calibri, Sans-Serif;font-
size: 12px;color:navy;"" align='left' nowrap='true'><div>" + rs.Fields(x).Value +
"</div></td>")
```

LINK

```
        txtstream.WriteLine("<td    style=""font-family:Calibri,   Sans-Serif;font-
size: 12px;color:navy;"" align='left' nowrap='true'><a href='" + rs.Fields(x).Value +
"'>" + rs.Fields(x).Value + "</a></td>")
```

LISTBOX

```
        txtstream.WriteLine("<td    style=""font-family:Calibri,   Sans-Serif;font-
size: 12px;color:navy;"" align='left' nowrap='true'><select multiple><option value =
"""" + rs.Fields(x).Value + """">" + rs.Fields(x).Value + "</option></select></td>")
```

SPAN

```
        txtstream.WriteLine("<td    style=""font-family:Calibri,   Sans-Serif;font-
size: 12px;color:navy;"" align='left' nowrap='true'><span>" + rs.Fields(x).Value +
"</span></td>")
```

TEXTAREA

```
        txtstream.WriteLine("<td    style=""font-family:Calibri,   Sans-Serif;font-
size: 12px;color:navy;"" align='left' nowrap='true'><textarea>" + rs.Fields(x).Value
+ "</textarea></td>")
```

TEXTBOX

```
        txtstream.WriteLine("<td    style=""font-family:Calibri,   Sans-Serif;font-
size: 12px;color:navy;"" align='left' nowrap='true'><input type=text value="""" +
rs.Fields(x).Value + """"></input></td>")
        Next
        txtstream.WriteLine("</tr>")
        rs.MoveNext
    Loop
    txtstream.WriteLine("</table>")
    txtstream.WriteLine("</body>")
    txtstream.WriteLine("</html>")
    txtstream.Close()
```

Vertical Reports

```
txtstream.WriteLine("<table border=0 cellspacing=3 cellpadding=3>")
For x = 0 to rs.Fields.Count-1
    txtstream.WriteLine("<tr><th    style=""    font-family:Calibri,    Sans-
Serif;font-size:   12px;color:darkred;""    align='left'   nowrap='nowrap'>"   +
rs.Fields(x).Name + "</th>")
        rs.MoveFirst()
        Do While(rs.EOF = false)
        txtstream.WriteLine("<td   style=""font-family:Calibri,   Sans-Serif;font-
size: 12px;color:navy;"">" + rs.Fields(x).Value + "</td>")
```

NONE

```
        txtstream.WriteLine("<td  style=""font-family:Calibri,  Sans-Serif;font-
size: 12px;color:navy;""  align='left'  nowrap='nowrap'>"  +  rs.Fields(x).Value  +
"</td>")
```

Button

```
        txtstream.WriteLine("<td    style=""font-family:Calibri,    Sans-Serif;font-
size: 12px;color:navy;""  align='left'  nowrap='true'><button  style='width:100%;'
value ='" + rs.Fields(x).Value + "'>" + rs.Fields(x).Value + "</button></td>")
```

Combobox

```
        txtstream.WriteLine("<td    style=""font-family:Calibri,    Sans-Serif;font-
size: 12px;color:navy;""  align='left'  nowrap='true'><select><option value = """ +
rs.Fields(x).Value + """>" + rs.Fields(x).Value + "</option></select></td>")
```

Div

```
        txtstream.WriteLine("<td  style=""font-family:Calibri, Sans-Serif;font-size:
12px;color:navy;""   align='left'   nowrap='true'><div>"   +   rs.Fields(x).Value   +
"</div></td>")
```

Link

```
txtstream.WriteLine("<td  style=""font-family:Calibri,  Sans-Serif;font-size:
12px;color:navy;"" align='left' nowrap='true'><a href='" + rs.Fields(x).Value + "'>"
+ rs.Fields(x).Value + "</a></td>")
```

Listbox

```
txtstream.WriteLine("<td  style=""font-family:Calibri,  Sans-Serif;font-size:
12px;color:navy;"" align='left' nowrap='true'><select multiple><option value = """
+ rs.Fields(x).Value + """>" + rs.Fields(x).Value + "</option></select></td>")
```

Span

```
txtstream.WriteLine("<td style=""font-family:Calibri, Sans-Serif;font-size:
12px;color:navy;""  align='left'  nowrap='true'><span>"  +  rs.Fields(x).Value  +
"</span></td>")
```

Textarea

```
txtstream.WriteLine("<td  style=""font-family:Calibri,  Sans-Serif;font-size:
12px;color:navy;""  align='left'  nowrap='true'><textarea>"  +  rs.Fields(x).Value  +
"</textarea></td>")
```

Textbox

```
        txtstream.WriteLine("<td   style=""font-family:Calibri,   Sans-Serif;font-
size: 12px;color:navy;""  align='left'  nowrap='true'><input  type=text  value="""  +
rs.Fields(x).Value + """></input></td>")
        rs.MoveNext
    Loop
  txtstream.WriteLine("</tr>")
Next
txtstream.WriteLine("</table>")
txtstream.WriteLine("</body>")
txtstream.WriteLine("</html>")
txtstream.Close()
```

Horizontal Tables

txtstream.WriteLine("<table   style='border:Double;border-width:1px;border-color:navy;' rules=all frames=both cellpadding=2 cellspacing=2 Width=0>")
txtstream.WriteLine("<tr>")
For x = 0 to rs.Fields.Count-1
txtstream.WriteLine("<th style="" font-family:Calibri, Sans-Serif;font-size: 12px;color:darkred;"" align='left' nowrap='nowrap'>" + rs.Fields(x).Name + "</th>")
Next
txtstream.WriteLine("</tr>")
Do While(rs.EOF = false)
txtstream.WriteLine("<tr>")
For x = 0 to rs.Fields.Count-1

NONE

txtstream.WriteLine("<td style=""font-family:Calibri, Sans-Serif;font-size: 12px;color:navy;"" align='left' nowrap='nowrap'>" + rs.Fields(x).Value + "</td>")

Button

txtstream.WriteLine("<td style=""font-family:Calibri, Sans-Serif;font-size: 12px;color:navy;"" align='left' nowrap='true'><button style='width:100%;' value ='" + rs.Fields(x).Value + "'>" + rs.Fields(x).Value + "</button></td>")

COMBOBOX

txtstream.WriteLine("<td style=""font-family:Calibri, Sans-Serif;font-size: 12px;color:navy;"" align='left' nowrap='true'><select><option value = """ + rs.Fields(x).Value + """>" + rs.Fields(x).Value + "</option></select></td>")

DIV

```
        txtstream.WriteLine("<td  style=""font-family:Calibri,  Sans-Serif;font-
size: 12px;color:navy;""" align='left' nowrap='true'><div>" + rs.Fields(x).Value +
"</div></td>")
```

LINK

```
        txtstream.WriteLine("<td  style=""font-family:Calibri,  Sans-Serif;font-
size: 12px;color:navy;""" align='left' nowrap='true'><a href='" + rs.Fields(x).Value +
"'>" + rs.Fields(x).Value + "</a></td>")
```

LISTBOX

```
        txtstream.WriteLine("<td  style=""font-family:Calibri,  Sans-Serif;font-
size: 12px;color:navy;""" align='left' nowrap='true'><select multiple><option value =
"""" + rs.Fields(x).Value + """">" + rs.Fields(x).Value + "</option></select></td>")
```

SPAN

```
        txtstream.WriteLine("<td  style=""font-family:Calibri,  Sans-Serif;font-
size: 12px;color:navy;""" align='left' nowrap='true'><span>" + rs.Fields(x).Value +
"</span></td>")
```

TEXTAREA

```
        txtstream.WriteLine("<td  style=""font-family:Calibri,  Sans-Serif;font-
size: 12px;color:navy;""" align='left' nowrap='true'><textarea>" + rs.Fields(x).Value
+ "</textarea></td>")
```

TEXTBOX

```
        txtstream.WriteLine("<td  style=""font-family:Calibri,  Sans-Serif;font-
size: 12px;color:navy;""" align='left' nowrap='true'><input type=text value="""" +
rs.Fields(x).Value + """"></input></td>")
    Next
    txtstream.WriteLine("</tr>")
    rs.MoveNext
Loop
txtstream.WriteLine("</table>")
txtstream.WriteLine("</body>")
```

```
txtstream.WriteLine("</html>")
txtstream.Close()
```

Vertical Tables

```
txtstream.WriteLine("<table        style='border:Double;border-width:1px;border-
color:navy;' rules=all frames=both cellpadding=2 cellspacing=2 Width=0>")
For x = 0 to rs.Fields.Count-1
        txtstream.WriteLine("<tr><th    style=""    font-family:Calibri,    Sans-
Serif;font-size:   12px;color:darkred;""    align='left'   nowrap='nowrap'>"   +
rs.Fields(x).Name + "</th>")
        rs.MoveFirst()
        Do While rs.EOF = false
        txtstream.WriteLine("<td   style=""font-family:Calibri,   Sans-Serif;font-
size: 12px;color:navy;"">" + rs.Fields(x).Value + "</td>")
```

NONE

```
        txtstream.WriteLine("<td   style=""font-family:Calibri,  Sans-Serif;font-
size:  12px;color:navy;""  align='left'  nowrap='nowrap'>"  +  rs.Fields(x).Value +
"</td>")
```

Button

```
        txtstream.WriteLine("<td   style=""font-family:Calibri,  Sans-Serif;font-
size: 12px;color:navy;""  align='left'  nowrap='true'><button  style='width:100%;'
value ='" + rs.Fields(x).Value + "'>" + rs.Fields(x).Value + "</button></td>")
```

Combobox

```
        txtstream.WriteLine("<td   style=""font-family:Calibri,  Sans-Serif;font-
size: 12px;color:navy;"" align='left' nowrap='true'><select><option value = """ +
rs.Fields(x).Value + """>" + rs.Fields(x).Value + "</option></select></td>")
```

Div

```
        txtstream.WriteLine("<td   style=""font-family:Calibri,   Sans-Serif;font-size:
12px;color:navy;"""   align='left'   nowrap='true'><div>"   +   rs.Fields(x).Value   +
"</div></td>")
```

Link

```
        txtstream.WriteLine("<td   style=""font-family:Calibri,   Sans-Serif;font-size:
12px;color:navy;""" align='left' nowrap='true'><a href='" + rs.Fields(x).Value + "'>"
+ rs.Fields(x).Value + "</a></td>")
```

Listbox

```
        txtstream.WriteLine("<td   style=""font-family:Calibri,   Sans-Serif;font-size:
12px;color:navy;""" align='left' nowrap='true'><select multiple><option value = """"
+ rs.Fields(x).Value + """">" + rs.Fields(x).Value + "</option></select></td>")
```

Span

```
        txtstream.WriteLine("<td style=""font-family:Calibri, Sans-Serif;font-size:
12px;color:navy;"""   align='left'   nowrap='true'><span>"   +   rs.Fields(x).Value   +
"</span></td>")
```

Textarea

```
        txtstream.WriteLine("<td   style=""font-family:Calibri,   Sans-Serif;font-size:
12px;color:navy;"""   align='left'   nowrap='true'><textarea>"   +   rs.Fields(x).Value   +
"</textarea></td>")
```

Textbox

```
        txtstream.WriteLine("<td    style=""font-family:Calibri,    Sans-Serif;font-
size: 12px;color:navy;"""   align='left'   nowrap='true'><input type=text value="""" +
rs.Fields(x).Value + """"></input></td>")
            rs.MoveNext
        Loop
        txtstream.WriteLine("</tr>")
    Next
    txtstream.WriteLine("</table>")
```

```
txtstream.WriteLine("</body>")
txtstream.WriteLine("</html>")
txtstream.Close()
```

HTML CODE

HAT CAN I SAY ABOUT HTML5 AND CSS THAT HASN'T BEEN SAID ALREADY? Well, I can say that it has come a long way since the 1990s.

```
Dim ws As Object =  CreateObject("WScript.Shell")
Dim fso As Object =  CreateObject("Scripting.FileSystemObject")
Dim  txtstream  As  Object  =fso.OpenTextFile(ws.CurrentDirectory  +
"\Products.html", 2, true, -2)
txtstream.WriteLine("<html>")
txtstream.WriteLine("<head>")
txtstream.WriteLine("<title>" + Tablename + "</title>")
#Add Stylesheet here
txtstream.WriteLine("<body>")
txtstream.WriteLine("</br>")
```

Horizontal Reports

```
txtstream.WriteLine("<table border=0 cellspacing=3 cellpadding=3>")
txtstream.WriteLine("<tr>")
```

```
      For x = 0 to rs.Fields.Count-1
         txtstream.WriteLine("<th style="""" font-family:Calibri,  Sans-Serif;font-size:
12px;color:darkred;"""   align='left'  nowrap='nowrap'>"  +  rs.Fields(x).Name  +
"</th>")

      txtstream.WriteLine("</tr>")
      Next
      Do While(rs.EOF = false)
         txtstream.WriteLine("<tr>")
         For x = 0 to rs.Fields.Count-1
```

NONE

```
            txtstream.WriteLine("<td   style="""font-family:Calibri,   Sans-Serif;font-
size: 12px;color:navy;"""   align='left'   nowrap='nowrap'>"  +  rs.Fields(x).Value  +
"</td>")
```

Button

```
            txtstream.WriteLine("<td   style="""font-family:Calibri,   Sans-Serif;font-
size: 12px;color:navy;"""  align='left'  nowrap='true'><button  style='width:100%;'
value ='" + rs.Fields(x).Value + "'>" + rs.Fields(x).Value + "</button></td>")
```

COMBOBOX

```
            txtstream.WriteLine("<td   style="""font-family:Calibri,   Sans-Serif;font-
size: 12px;color:navy;"""  align='left'  nowrap='true'><select><option value = """" +
rs.Fields(x).Value + """">" + rs.Fields(x).Value + "</option></select></td>")
```

DIV

```
            txtstream.WriteLine("<td   style="""font-family:Calibri,   Sans-Serif;font-
size: 12px;color:navy;"""  align='left'  nowrap='true'><div>"  +  rs.Fields(x).Value  +
"</div></td>")
```

LINK

```
        txtstream.WriteLine("<td    style="""font-family:Calibri,   Sans-Serif;font-
size: 12px;color:navy;""" align='left' nowrap='true'><a href='"" + rs.Fields(x).Value +
"'>" + rs.Fields(x).Value + "</a></td>")
```

LISTBOX

```
        txtstream.WriteLine("<td    style="""font-family:Calibri,   Sans-Serif;font-
size: 12px;color:navy;""" align='left' nowrap='true'><select multiple><option value =
"""" + rs.Fields(x).Value + """">" + rs.Fields(x).Value + "</option></select></td>")
```

SPAN

```
        txtstream.WriteLine("<td    style="""font-family:Calibri,   Sans-Serif;font-
size: 12px;color:navy;""" align='left' nowrap='true'><span>" + rs.Fields(x).Value +
"</span></td>")
```

TEXTAREA

```
        txtstream.WriteLine("<td    style="""font-family:Calibri,   Sans-Serif;font-
size: 12px;color:navy;""" align='left' nowrap='true'><textarea>" + rs.Fields(x).Value
+ "</textarea></td>")
```

TEXTBOX

```
        txtstream.WriteLine("<td    style="""font-family:Calibri,   Sans-Serif;font-
size: 12px;color:navy;""" align='left' nowrap='true'><input type=text value="""" +
rs.Fields(x).Value + """"></input></td>")
        Next
        txtstream.WriteLine("</tr>")
        rs.MoveNext
    Loop
    txtstream.WriteLine("</table>")
    txtstream.WriteLine("</body>")
    txtstream.WriteLine("</html>")
    txtstream.Close()
```

Vertical Reports

```
txtstream.WriteLine("<table border=0 cellspacing=3 cellpadding=3>")
For x = 0 to rs.Fields.Count-1
        txtstream.WriteLine("<tr><th    style=""    font-family:Calibri,    Sans-
Serif;font-size:    12px;color:darkred;""    align='left'    nowrap='nowrap'>"    +
rs.Fields(x).Name + "</th>")
        rs.MoveFirst()
        Do While(rs.EOF = false)
        txtstream.WriteLine("<td    style=""font-family:Calibri,    Sans-Serif;font-
size: 12px;color:navy;"">" + rs.Fields(x).Value + "</td>")
```

NONE

```
        txtstream.WriteLine("<td    style=""font-family:Calibri,    Sans-Serif;font-
size:  12px;color:navy;""  align='left'  nowrap='nowrap'>"  +  rs.Fields(x).Value  +
"</td>")
```

Button

```
        txtstream.WriteLine("<td    style=""font-family:Calibri,    Sans-Serif;font-
size:  12px;color:navy;""  align='left'  nowrap='true'><button  style='width:100%;'
value ='" + rs.Fields(x).Value + "'>" + rs.Fields(x).Value + "</button></td>")
```

Combobox

```
        txtstream.WriteLine("<td    style=""font-family:Calibri,    Sans-Serif;font-
size: 12px;color:navy;""  align='left'  nowrap='true'><select><option value = """"  +
rs.Fields(x).Value + """">" + rs.Fields(x).Value + "</option></select></td>")
```

Div

```
        txtstream.WriteLine("<td  style=""font-family:Calibri,  Sans-Serif;font-size:
12px;color:navy;""    align='left'    nowrap='true'><div>"    +    rs.Fields(x).Value    +
"</div></td>")
```

Link

```
txtstream.WriteLine("<td    style=""font-family:Calibri,    Sans-Serif;font-size:
12px;color:navy;""" align='left' nowrap='true'><a href='" + rs.Fields(x).Value + "'>"
+ rs.Fields(x).Value + "</a></td>")
```

Listbox

```
txtstream.WriteLine("<td    style=""font-family:Calibri,    Sans-Serif;font-size:
12px;color:navy;""" align='left' nowrap='true'><select multiple><option value = """"
+ rs.Fields(x).Value + """">" + rs.Fields(x).Value + "</option></select></td>")
```

Span

```
txtstream.WriteLine("<td style=""font-family:Calibri, Sans-Serif;font-size:
12px;color:navy;""" align='left' nowrap='true'><span>" + rs.Fields(x).Value +
"</span></td>")
```

Textarea

```
txtstream.WriteLine("<td    style=""font-family:Calibri,    Sans-Serif;font-size:
12px;color:navy;""" align='left' nowrap='true'><textarea>" + rs.Fields(x).Value +
"</textarea></td>")
```

Textbox

```
txtstream.WriteLine("<td    style=""font-family:Calibri,    Sans-Serif;font-
size: 12px;color:navy;""" align='left' nowrap='true'><input type=text value=""""" +
rs.Fields(x).Value + """"></input></td>")
        rs.MoveNext
       Loop
    txtstream.WriteLine("</tr>")
Next
txtstream.WriteLine("</table>")
txtstream.WriteLine("</body>")
txtstream.WriteLine("</html>")
txtstream.Close()
```

Horizontal Tables

```
txtstream.WriteLine("<table     style='border:Double;border-width:1px;border-
color:navy;' rules=all frames=both cellpadding=2 cellspacing=2 Width=0>")
txtstream.WriteLine("<tr>")
For x = 0 to rs.Fields.Count-1
    txtstream.WriteLine("<th style="" font-family:Calibri, Sans-Serif;font-size:
12px;color:darkred;""  align='left'  nowrap='nowrap'>" +  rs.Fields(x).Name +
"</th>")
Next
txtstream.WriteLine("</tr>")
Do While(rs.EOF = false)
    txtstream.WriteLine("<tr>")
    For x = 0 to rs.Fields.Count-1
```

NONE

```
        txtstream.WriteLine("<td   style=""font-family:Calibri,   Sans-Serif;font-
size: 12px;color:navy;""  align='left'  nowrap='nowrap'>"  +  rs.Fields(x).Value +
"</td>")
```

Button

```
        txtstream.WriteLine("<td   style=""font-family:Calibri,   Sans-Serif;font-
size: 12px;color:navy;""  align='left'  nowrap='true'><button  style='width:100%;'
value ='" + rs.Fields(x).Value + "'>" + rs.Fields(x).Value + "</button></td>")
```

COMBOBOX

```
        txtstream.WriteLine("<td   style=""font-family:Calibri,   Sans-Serif;font-
size: 12px;color:navy;""  align='left' nowrap='true'><select><option value = """ +
rs.Fields(x).Value + """>" + rs.Fields(x).Value + "</option></select></td>")
```

DIV

```
        txtstream.WriteLine("<td   style=""font-family:Calibri,   Sans-Serif;font-
size: 12px;color:navy;""  align='left' nowrap='true'><div>" + rs.Fields(x).Value +
"</div></td>")
```

LINK

```
        txtstream.WriteLine("<td style="""font-family:Calibri, Sans-Serif;font-
size: 12px;color:navy;""" align='left' nowrap='true'><a href='" + rs.Fields(x).Value +
"'>" + rs.Fields(x).Value + "</a></td>")
```

LISTBOX

```
        txtstream.WriteLine("<td style="""font-family:Calibri, Sans-Serif;font-
size: 12px;color:navy;""" align='left' nowrap='true'><select multiple><option value =
"""" + rs.Fields(x).Value + """">" + rs.Fields(x).Value + "</option></select></td>")
```

SPAN

```
        txtstream.WriteLine("<td style="""font-family:Calibri, Sans-Serif;font-
size: 12px;color:navy;""" align='left' nowrap='true'><span>" + rs.Fields(x).Value +
"</span></td>")
```

TEXTAREA

```
        txtstream.WriteLine("<td style="""font-family:Calibri, Sans-Serif;font-
size: 12px;color:navy;""" align='left' nowrap='true'><textarea>" + rs.Fields(x).Value
+ "</textarea></td>")
```

TEXTBOX

```
        txtstream.WriteLine("<td style="""font-family:Calibri, Sans-Serif;font-
size: 12px;color:navy;""" align='left' nowrap='true'><input type=text value="""" +
rs.Fields(x).Value + """"></input></td>")
    Next
    txtstream.WriteLine("</tr>")
    rs.MoveNext
Loop
txtstream.WriteLine("</table>")
txtstream.WriteLine("</body>")
txtstream.WriteLine("</html>")
txtstream.Close()
```

Vertical Tables

txtstream.WriteLine("<table   style='border:Double;border-width:1px;border-color:navy;' rules=all frames=both cellpadding=2 cellspacing=2 Width=0>")
For x = 0 to rs.Fields.Count-1
txtstream.WriteLine("<tr><th   style=""   font-family:Calibri,   Sans-Serif;font-size: 12px;color:darkred;""   align='left'   nowrap='nowrap'>"   + rs.Fields(x).Name + "</th>")
rs.MoveFirst()
Do While rs.EOF = false
txtstream.WriteLine("<td   style=""font-family:Calibri,   Sans-Serif;font-size: 12px;color:navy;"">" + rs.Fields(x).Value + "</td>")

NONE

txtstream.WriteLine("<td   style=""font-family:Calibri,   Sans-Serif;font-size: 12px;color:navy;""   align='left'   nowrap='nowrap'>"   + rs.Fields(x).Value   + "</td>")

Button

txtstream.WriteLine("<td   style=""font-family:Calibri,   Sans-Serif;font-size: 12px;color:navy;""   align='left'   nowrap='true'><button style='width:100%;' value ='" + rs.Fields(x).Value + "'>" + rs.Fields(x).Value + "</button></td>")

Combobox

txtstream.WriteLine("<td   style=""font-family:Calibri,   Sans-Serif;font-size: 12px;color:navy;""   align='left'   nowrap='true'><select><option value = """ + rs.Fields(x).Value + """>" + rs.Fields(x).Value + "</option></select></td>")

Div

txtstream.WriteLine("<td   style=""font-family:Calibri,   Sans-Serif;font-size: 12px;color:navy;""   align='left'   nowrap='true'> "   +   rs.Fields(x).Value   + " </td>")

Link

```
txtstream.WriteLine("<td   style=""font-family:Calibri,   Sans-Serif;font-size:
12px;color:navy;"" align='left' nowrap='true'><a href='" + rs.Fields(x).Value + "'>"
+ rs.Fields(x).Value + "</a></td>")
```

Listbox

```
txtstream.WriteLine("<td   style=""font-family:Calibri,   Sans-Serif;font-size:
12px;color:navy;"" align='left' nowrap='true'><select multiple><option value = """"
+ rs.Fields(x).Value + """">" + rs.Fields(x).Value + "</option></select></td>")
```

Span

```
txtstream.WriteLine("<td style=""font-family:Calibri, Sans-Serif;font-size:
12px;color:navy;""  align='left' nowrap='true'><span>" + rs.Fields(x).Value +
"</span></td>")
```

Textarea

```
txtstream.WriteLine("<td   style=""font-family:Calibri,   Sans-Serif;font-size:
12px;color:navy;"" align='left' nowrap='true'><textarea>" + rs.Fields(x).Value +
"</textarea></td>")
```

Textbox

```
        txtstream.WriteLine("<td   style=""font-family:Calibri,   Sans-Serif;font-
size: 12px;color:navy;"" align='left' nowrap='true'><input type=text value="""" +
rs.Fields(x).Value + """"></input></td>")
            rs.MoveNext
        Loop
        txtstream.WriteLine("</tr>")
    Next
    txtstream.WriteLine("</table>")
    txtstream.WriteLine("</body>")
    txtstream.WriteLine("</html>")
    txtstream.Close()
```

DELIMITED FILES

T

HERE ARE MANY DIFFERENT KINDS OF DELIMITED FILES. The ones we are going to be using are the most common ones. And by Common, this will include:

- Colon Delimited
- Comma Delimited
- Exclamation Delimited
- Semi-Colon Delimited
- Tab Delimited
- Tilde Delimited

Essentially, the only differences in the code is how the delimiter is used, but the code examples are also going to show you how the information can be arranged in both Horizontal and Vertical Views.

Colon Delimited Horizontal View

```
Dim ws As Object = CreateObject("WScript.Shell")
Dim fso As Object = CreateObject("Scripting.FileSystemObject")
Dim  txtstream  As  Object  =fso.OpenTextFile(ws.CurrentDirectory  +
"\Products.txt", 2, true, -2)
tstr= ""
For x = 0 to rs.Fields.Count-1
  if tstr <> "" Then
    tstr = tstr + ":"
  End If
  tstr = tstr + rs.Fields(x).Name
Next
txtstream.Writeline(tstr)
tstr = ""
rs.MoveFirst()
Do While(rs.EOF = false)
  For x = 0 to rs.Fields.Count-1
    if tstr <> "" Then
      tstr = tstr + ":"
    End If
    tstr = tstr + chr(34) + rs.Fields(x).Value + chr(34)
  Next
  txtstream.Writeline(tstr)
  tstr = ""
  rs.MoveNext
Loop
```

Colon Delimited Vertical View

```
For x = 0 to rs.Fields.Count-1
  tstr = rs.Fields(x).Name
  rs.MoveFirst()
  Do While(rs.EOF = false)
    if tstr <> "" Then
      tstr = tstr + ":"
    End If
    tstr = tstr + chr(34) + rs.Fields(x).Value + chr(34)
    rs.MoveNext
```

```
      Loop
      txtstream.Writeline(tstr)
      tstr = ""
   Next
   txtstream.Close
```

Comma Delimited Horizontal

```
   Dim ws As Object =  CreateObject("WScript.Shell")
   Dim fso As Object =  CreateObject("Scripting.FileSystemObject")
   Dim    txtstream    As    Object    =fso.OpenTextFile(ws.CurrentDirectory    +
"\Products.csv", 2, true, -2)
   tstr= ""
   For x = 0 to rs.Fields.Count-1
     if tstr <> "" Then
       tstr = tstr + ","
     End If
     tstr = tstr + rs.Fields(x).Name
   Next
   txtstream.Writeline(tstr)
   tstr = ""
   rs.MoveFirst()
   Do While(rs.EOF = false)
     For x = 0 to rs.Fields.Count-1
       if tstr <> "" Then
         tstr = tstr + ","
       End If
       tstr = tstr + chr(34) + rs.Fields(x).Value + chr(34)
     Next
     txtstream.Writeline(tstr)
     tstr = ""
     rs.MoveNext
   Loop
```

Comma Delimited Vertical

```
   Dim ws As Object =  CreateObject("WScript.Shell")
   Dim fso As Object =  CreateObject("Scripting.FileSystemObject")
```

```
        Dim txtstream As Object =fso.OpenTextFile(ws.CurrentDirectory +
"\Products.csv", 2, true, -2)

        For x = 0 to rs.Fields.Count-1
            tstr = rs.Fields(x).Name
            rs.MoveFirst()
            Do While(rs.EOF = false)
                if tstr <> "" Then
                    tstr = tstr + ","
                End If
                tstr = tstr + chr(34) + rs.Fields(x).Value + chr(34)
                rs.MoveNext
            Loop
            txtstream.Writeline(tstr)
            tstr = ""
        Next
        txtstream.Close
```

Exclamation Delimited Horizontal

```
        Dim ws As Object =  CreateObject("WScript.Shell")
        Dim fso As Object =  CreateObject("Scripting.FileSystemObject")
        Dim    txtstream    As    Object    =fso.OpenTextFile(ws.CurrentDirectory    +
"\Products.txt", 2, true, -2)
        tstr= ""
        For x = 0 to rs.Fields.Count-1
            if tstr <> "" Then
                tstr = tstr + "!"
            End If
            tstr = tstr + rs.Fields(x).Name
        Next
        txtstream.Writeline(tstr)
        tstr = ""
        rs.MoveFirst()
        Do While(rs.EOF = false)
            For x = 0 to rs.Fields.Count-1
                if tstr <> "" Then
```

```
            tstr = tstr + "!"
         End If
         tstr = tstr + chr(34) + rs.Fields(x).Value + chr(34)
      Next
      txtstream.Writeline(tstr)
      tstr = ""
      rs.MoveNext
   Loop
```

Exclamation Delimited Vertical

```
      Dim ws As Object = CreateObject("WScript.Shell")
      Dim fso As Object = CreateObject("Scripting.FileSystemObject")
      Dim   txtstream   As   Object   =fso.OpenTextFile(ws.CurrentDirectory   +
"\Products.txt", 2, true, -2)

      For x = 0 to rs.Fields.Count-1
         tstr = rs.Fields(x).Name
         rs.MoveFirst()
         Do While(rs.EOF = false)
            if tstr <> "" Then
               tstr = tstr + "!"
            End If
            tstr = tstr + chr(34) + rs.Fields(x).Value + chr(34)
            rs.MoveNext
         Loop
         txtstream.Writeline(tstr)
         tstr = ""
      Next
      txtstream.Close
```

Semi Colon Delimited Horizontal

```
      Dim ws As Object = CreateObject("WScript.Shell")
      Dim fso As Object = CreateObject("Scripting.FileSystemObject")
      Dim   txtstream   As   Object   =fso.OpenTextFile(ws.CurrentDirectory   +
"\Products.txt", 2, true, -2)
      tstr= ""
```

```
For x = 0 to rs.Fields.Count-1
   if tstr <> "" Then
      tstr = tstr + ";"
   End If
   tstr = tstr + rs.Fields(x).Name
Next
txtstream.Writeline(tstr)
tstr = ""
rs.MoveFirst()
Do While(rs.EOF = false)
   For x = 0 to rs.Fields.Count-1
      if tstr <> "" Then
         tstr = tstr + ";"
      End If
      tstr = tstr + chr(34) + rs.Fields(x).Value + chr(34)
   Next
   txtstream.Writeline(tstr)
   tstr = ""
   rs.MoveNext
Loop
```

Semi Colon Delimited Vertical

```
Dim ws As Object =  CreateObject("WScript.Shell")
Dim fso As Object =  CreateObject("Scripting.FileSystemObject")
Dim  txtstream  As  Object  =fso.OpenTextFile(ws.CurrentDirectory  +
"\Products.txt", 2, true, -2)

For x = 0 to rs.Fields.Count-1
   tstr = rs.Fields(x).Name
   rs.MoveFirst()
   Do While(rs.EOF = false)
      if tstr <> "" Then
         tstr = tstr + ";"
      End If
      tstr = tstr + chr(34) + rs.Fields(x).Value + chr(34)
      rs.MoveNext
   Loop
   txtstream.Writeline(tstr)
```

```
      tstr = ""
   Next
   txtstream.Close
```

Tab Delimited Horizontal

```
   Dim ws As Object = CreateObject("WScript.Shell")
   Dim fso As Object = CreateObject("Scripting.FileSystemObject")
   Dim  txtstream  As  Object  =fso.OpenTextFile(ws.CurrentDirectory  +
"\Products.txt", 2, true, -2)
   tstr= ""

   For x = 0 to rs.Fields.Count-1
     if tstr <> "" Then
        tstr = tstr + vbTab
     End If
     tstr = tstr + rs.Fields(x).Name
   Next
   txtstream.Writeline(tstr)
   tstr = ""
   rs.MoveFirst()
   Do While(rs.EOF = false)
     For x = 0 to rs.Fields.Count-1
        if tstr <> "" Then
           tstr = tstr + vbTab
        End If
        tstr = tstr + chr(34) + rs.Fields(x).Value + chr(34)
     Next
     txtstream.Writeline(tstr)
     tstr = ""
     rs.MoveNext
   Loop
```

Tab Delimited Vertical

```
   Dim ws As Object = CreateObject("WScript.Shell")
   Dim fso As Object = CreateObject("Scripting.FileSystemObject")
   Dim  txtstream  As  Object  =fso.OpenTextFile(ws.CurrentDirectory  +
"\Products.txt", 2, true, -2)
```

```
For x = 0 to rs.Fields.Count-1
   tstr = rs.Fields(x).Name
   rs.MoveFirst()
   Do While(rs.EOF = false)
      if tstr <> "" Then
         tstr = tstr + vbTab
      End If
      tstr = tstr + chr(34) + rs.Fields(x).Value + chr(34)
      rs.MoveNext
   Loop
   txtstream.Writeline(tstr)
   tstr = ""
Next
txtstream.Close
```

Tilde Delimited Horizontal

```
Dim ws As Object = CreateObject("WScript.Shell")
Dim fso As Object = CreateObject("Scripting.FileSystemObject")
Dim txtstream As Object =fso.OpenTextFile(ws.CurrentDirectory +
"\Products.txt", 2, true, -2)
tstr= ""
For x = 0 to rs.Fields.Count-1
   if tstr <> "" Then
      tstr = tstr + "~"
   End If
   tstr = tstr + rs.Fields(x).Name
Next
txtstream.Writeline(tstr)
tstr = ""
rs.MoveFirst()
Do While(rs.EOF = false)
   For x = 0 to rs.Fields.Count-1
      if tstr <> "" Then
         tstr = tstr + "~"
      End If
```

```
      tstr = tstr + chr(34) + rs.Fields(x).Value + chr(34)
   Next
   txtstream.Writeline(tstr)
   tstr = ""
   rs.MoveNext
Loop
```

Tilde Delimited Vertical

```
Dim ws As Object = CreateObject("WScript.Shell")
Dim fso As Object = CreateObject("Scripting.FileSystemObject")
Dim txtstream As Object =fso.OpenTextFile(ws.CurrentDirectory +
"\Products.txt", 2, true, -2)
For x = 0 to rs.Fields.Count-1
   tstr = rs.Fields(x).Name
   rs.MoveFirst()
   Do While(rs.EOF = false)
      if tstr <> "" Then
         tstr = tstr + "~"
      End If
      tstr = tstr + chr(34) + rs.Fields(x).Value + chr(34)
      rs.MoveNext
   Loop
   txtstream.Writeline(tstr)
   tstr = ""
Next
txtstream.Close
```

XML FILES

n this section of the book, we're going to be Coding for the creation of Attribute XML Element XML, Element XML for XSL and Schema XML

Attribute XML Using A Text file

```
ws  = CreateObject("WScript.Shell")
fso  = CreateObject("Scripting.FileSystemObject")
txtstream = fso.OpenTextFile("C:\Products.xml", 2, true, -2)
txtstream.WriteLine("<?xml version='1.0' encoding='iso-8859-1'?>")
txtstream.WriteLine("<data>")
rs.MoveFirst()
Do While(rs.EOF = false)
   txtstream.WriteLine("<Products>")
   For x in range(rs.Fields.Count):
     txtstream.WriteLine("<property name = """ + rs.Fields(x).Name + """
value=""" + rs.Fields(x).value + """/>")
   Next
   txtstream.WriteLine("</Products>")
   rs.MoveNext()
   Loop
```

```
txtstream.WriteLine("</data>")
txtstream.Close
```

Attribute XML Using the DOM

```
Dim xmldoc as Object = CreateObject("MSXML2.DOMDocument")
Dim pi As Object = xmldoc.CreateProcessingInstruction("xml",
"version='1.0' encoding='ISO-8859-1'")
Dim oRoot As Object = xmldoc.CreateElement("data")
xmldoc.AppendChild(pi)
Do While rs.EOF = false
  Dim oNode As Object = xmldoc.CreateNode(1, "Products", "")
  for x in range(rs.Fields.Count):
    Dim oNode1 As Object = xmldoc.CreateNode(1, "Property", "")
    Dim oAtt As Object = = xmldoc.CreateAttribute("NAME")
    oAtt.Value = rs.Fields(x).Name
    oNode1.Attributes.SetNamedItem(oAtt)
    Dim oAtt As Object = = xmldoc.CreateAttribute("DATATYPE")
    oAtt.Value = str(rs.Fields(x).Type.Name))
    oNode1.Attributes.SetNamedItem(oAtt)
    Dim oAtt As Object = = xmldoc.CreateAttribute("SIZE")
    oAtt.Value = str(rs.Fields(x).Value.)
    oNode1.Attributes.SetNamedItem(oAtt)
    Dim oAtt As Object = = xmldoc.CreateAttribute("Value")
    oAtt.Value = GetValue(prop, obj)
    oNode1.Attributes.SetNamedItem(oAtt)
    oNode.AppendChild(oNode1)
  Next
  oRoot.AppendChild(oNode)
Loop
xmldoc.AppendChild(oRoot)
Dim ws As Object = CreateObject("WScript.Shell")
xmldoc.Save(ws.CurrentDirectory + "\\Products.xml")
```

Element XML Using A Text file

```
Dim ws As Object =  CreateObject("WScript.Shell")
Dim fso As Object =  CreateObject("Scripting.FileSystemObject")
Dim   txtstream   As   Object   =fso.OpenTextFile(ws.CurrentDirectory   +
"\Products.txt", 2, true, -2)
txtstream.WriteLine("<?xml version='1.0' encoding='iso-8859-1'?>")
txtstream.WriteLine("<data>")
rs.MoveFirst
Do While(rs.EOF = false)
   txtstream.WriteLine("<Products>")
   For x = 0 to rs.Fields.Count-1
      txtstream.WriteLine("<" + rs.Fields(x).Name + ">" + rs.Fields(x).Value +
"</" + rs.Fields(x).Name + ">")
   Next
   txtstream.WriteLine("</Products>")
   rs.MoveNext()
Loop
txtstream.WriteLine("</data>")
txtstream.close()
```

Element XML Using the DOM

```
Dim xmldoc as Object   = CreateObject("MSXML2.DOMDocument")
 Dim pi As Object = xmldoc.CreateProcessingInstruction("xml",
"version='1.0' encoding='ISO-8859-1'")

Dim oRoot As Object  = xmldoc.CreateElement("data")
xmldoc.AppendChild(pi)
Do While rs.EOF  = false
   Dim oNode As Object  = xmldoc.CreateNode(1, "Products", "")
   for x = 0 to rs.Fields.Count -1
       Dim oNode1 As Object = xmldoc.CreateNode(1, rs.Fields(x),Name, "")
       oNode1.Text = str(rs.Fields(x).Value)
       Call oNode.AppendChild(oNode1)
   Next
   Call oRoot.AppendChild(oNode)
   rs.MoveNext
Loop
```

```
        Call xmldoc.AppendChild(oRoot)
        Dim ws As Object = CreateObject("WScript.Shell")
        xmldoc.Save(ws.CurrentDirectory + "\\Products.xml")
```

Element XML FOR XSL Using A Text File

```
        Dim ws As Object = CreateObject("WScript.Shell")
        Dim fso As Object = CreateObject("Scripting.FileSystemObject")
        Dim    txtstream    As    Object    =fso.OpenTextFile(ws.CurrentDirectory    +
"\Products.txt", 2, true, -2)
        txtstream.WriteLine("<?xml version='1.0' encoding='iso-8859-1'?>")
        txtstream.WriteLine("<?xml-stylesheet        type='Text/xsl'        href='"    +
ws.CurrentDirectory + "\Products.xsl"?>
        txtstream.WriteLine("<?xml version='1.0' encoding='iso-8859-1'?>")
        txtstream.WriteLine("<data>")
        rs.MoveFirst
        Do While(rs.EOF = false)
           txtstream.WriteLine("<Products>")
           For x = 0 to rs.Fields.Count-1
              txtstream.WriteLine("<" + rs.Fields(x).Name + ">" + rs.Fields(x).Value +
"</" + rs.Fields(x).Name + ">")
           Next
           txtstream.WriteLine("</Products>")
           rs.MoveNext()
        Loop
        txtstream.WriteLine("</data>")
        txtstream.close()
```

Element XML FOR XSL Using The DOM

```
     Dim xmldoc as Object  = CreateObject("MSXML2.DOMDocument")
      Dim pi As Object = xmldoc.CreateProcessingInstruction("xml", "version='1.0'
      encoding='ISO-8859-1'")
     Dim    pii    As    Object    xmldoc.CreateProcessingInstruction("xml-stylesheet",
"type='text/xsl' href='Process.xsl'")
     Dim oRoot As Object = xmldoc.CreateElement("data")
     xmldoc.AppendChild(pi)
     xmldoc.AppendChild(pii)
     Do While rs.EOF = false
```

```
    Dim oNode As Object  = xmldoc.CreateNode(1, "Products", "")
    for x = 0 to rs.Fields.Count -1
       Dim oNode1 As Object = xmldoc.CreateNode(1, rs.Fields(x),Name, "")
       oNode1.Text = str(rs.Fields(x).Value)
       Call oNode.AppendChild(oNode1)
    Next
    Call oRoot.AppendChild(oNode)
    rs.MoveNext
Loop
Call xmldoc.AppendChild(oRoot)
Dim ws As Object =  CreateObject("WScript.Shell")
xmldoc.Save(ws.CurrentDirectory + "\\Products.xml")
```

Schema XML Using A Text File

```
Dim ws As Object =  CreateObject("WScript.Shell")
Dim fso As Object =  CreateObject("Scripting.FileSystemObject")
Dim   txtstream   As   Object   =fso.OpenTextFile(ws.CurrentDirectory   +
"\Products.txt", 2, true, -2)
txtstream.WriteLine("<?xml version='1.0' encoding='iso-8859-1'?>")
txtstream.WriteLine("<data>")
rs.MoveFirst
Do While(rs.EOF = false)
   txtstream.WriteLine("<Products>")
   For x = 0 to rs.Fields.Count-1
      txtstream.WriteLine("<" + rs.Fields(x).Name + ">" + rs.Fields(x).Value +
"</" + rs.Fields(x).Name + ">")
   Next
   txtstream.WriteLine("</Products>")
   rs.MoveNext()
Loop
txtstream.WriteLine("</data>")
txtstream.close()
rs1 = CreateObject("ADODB.Recordset")
rs1.ActiveConnection         =         "Provider=MSDAOSP;         Data
Source=msxml2.DSOControl"
rs1.Open(ws.CurrentDirectory + "\Products.xml")
```

```
        If (fso.FileExists(ws.CurrentDirectory + "\Products_Schema.xml") = true)
Then
            fso.DeleteFile(ws.CurrentDirectory + "\Products_Schema.xml")


        rs.Save(ws.CurrentDirectory + "\Products_Schema.xml", 1)
```

Schema XML Using the DOM

```
        Dim xmldoc as Object   = CreateObject("MSXML2.DOMDocument")
        Dim pi As Object = xmldoc.CreateProcessingInstruction("xml",
    "version='1.0' encoding='ISO-8859-1'")
        Dim oRoot As Object  = xmldoc.CreateElement("data")
        xmldoc.AppendChild(pi)
        Do While rs.EOF = false
            Dim oNode As Object  = xmldoc.CreateNode(1, "Products", "")
          for x = 0 to rs.Fields.Count -1
              Dim oNode1 As Object = xmldoc.CreateNode(1, rs.Fields(x),Name, "")
              oNode1.Text = str(rs.Fields(x).Value)
              Call oNode.AppendChild(oNode1)
          Next
          Call oRoot.AppendChild(oNode)
          rs.MoveNext
        Loop
        Call xmldoc.AppendChild(oRoot)
        Dim ws As Object =  CreateObject("WScript.Shell")
        xmldoc.Save(ws.CurrentDirectory + "\\Products.xml")




        Dim rs1 As Object = CreateObject("ADODB.Recordset")
        rs1.ActiveConnection = "Provider=MSDAOSP; Data
Source=msxml2.DSOControl"
        rs1.Open(ws.CurrentDirectory + "\Products.xml")


        If (fso.FileExists(ws.CurrentDirectory + "\Products_Schema.xml") = true)
Then
            fso.DeleteFile(ws.CurrentDirectory + "\Products_Schema.xml")
```

```
rs.Save(ws.CurrentDirectory + "\Products_Schema.xml", 1)
```

EXCEL CODING EXAMPLES

ELOW ARE SOME EXAMPLES OF ADO DRIVING EXCEL VISUAL RENDERINGS.

Excel Code in Horizontal Format using a CSV File

```
Dim ws As Object = CreateObject("WScript.Shell")
Dim fso As Object = CreateObject("Scripting.FileSystemObject")
Dim   txtstream   As   Object   =fso.OpenTextFile(ws.CurrentDirectory   +
"\Products.csv", 2, true, -2)
tstr= ""


For x = 0 to rs.Fields.Count-1
  if tstr <> "" Then
     tstr = tstr + ","
  End If
  tstr = tstr + rs.Fields(x).Name
Next
txtstream.Writeline(tstr)
tstr = ""
rs.MoveFirst()
Do While(rs.EOF = false)
```

```
      For x = 0 to rs.Fields.Count-1
        if tstr <> "" Then
           tstr = tstr + ","
        End If
        tstr = tstr + chr(34) + rs.Fields(x).Value + chr(34)
      Next
      txtstream.Writeline(tstr)
      tstr = ""
      rs.MoveNext
   Loop
```

Excel Code in Vertical Format using a CSV File

```
   Dim ws As Object =  CreateObject("WScript.Shell")
   Dim fso As Object =  CreateObject("Scripting.FileSystemObject")
   Dim   txtstream   As   Object   =fso.OpenTextFile(ws.CurrentDirectory   +
"\Products.csv", 2, true, -2)
   tstr= ""
   For x = 0 to rs.Fields.Count-1
     tstr = rs.Fields(x).Name
     rs.MoveFirst()
     Do While(rs.EOF = false)
       if tstr <> "" Then
          tstr = tstr + ","
       End If
       tstr = tstr + chr(34) + rs.Fields(x).Value + chr(34)
       rs.MoveNext
     Loop
     txtstream.Writeline(tstr)
     tstr = ""
   Next
   txtstream.Close

   ws.Run(ws.CurrentDirectory + "\Products.csv")
```

Excel using Horizontal Format Automation Code

```
   Dim oExcel As Object = CreateObject("Excel.Application")
   oExcel.Visible = true
```

```
Dim wb As Object  As Object = oExcel.Workbooks.Add()
Dim ws As Object = wb.WorkSheets(1)
ws.Name = "Products"
y=2
For x = 0 to rs.Fields.Count-1
   ws.Cells.Item(1, x+1) = rs.Fields(x).Name
Next
rs.MoveFirst()
Do While rs.EOF = False
   For x = 0 to rs.Fields.Count-1
      ws.Cells.Item(y, x +1) = rs.Fields(x).Value
   Next
   y=y+1
   rs.MoveNext
Loop

ws.Columns.HorizontalAlignment = -4131
iret = ws.Columns.AutoFit()
```

Excel using Vertical Format Automation Code

```
oExcel = CreateObject("Excel.Application")
oExcel.Visible = true
wb = oExcel.Workbooks.Add()
Dim ws As Object = wb.WorkSheets(1)
ws.Name = "Products"
y=2
For x = 0 to rs.Fields.Count-1
   ws.Cells.Item(x+1, 1) = rs.Fields(x).Name
Next
rs.MoveFirst()
Do While rs.EOF = False
   For x = 0 to rs.Fields.Count-1
      ws.Cells.Item(x +1, y) = rs.Fields(x).Value
   Next
   y=y+1
   rs.MoveNext
Loop
```

```
ws.Columns.HorizontalAlignment = -4131
iret = ws.Columns.AutoFit()
```

Excel Spreadsheet Example

```
Dim ws As Object = CreateObject("WScript.Shell")
Dim fso As Object = CreateObject("Scripting.FileSystemObject")
Dim   txtstream   As   Object   =fso.OpenTextFile(ws.CurrentDirectory   +
"\\ProcessExcel.xml", 2, true, -2)
txtstream.WriteLine("<?xml version='1.0'?>")
txtstream.WriteLine("<?mso-application progid='Excel.Sheet'?>")
txtstream.WriteLine("<Workbook                xmlns='urn:schemas-microsoft-
com:office:spreadsheet'        xmlns:o='urn:schemas-microsoft-com:office:office'
xmlns:x='urn:schemas-microsoft-com:office:excel'        xmlns:ss='urn:schemas-
microsoft-com:office:spreadsheet'        xmlns:html='http://www.w3.org/TR/REC-
html40'>")
txtstream.WriteLine(" <DocumentProperties    xmlns='urn:schemas-microsoft-
com:office:office'>")
txtstream.WriteLine("          <Author>Windows User</Author>")
txtstream.WriteLine("          <LastAuthor>Windows User</LastAuthor>")
txtstream.WriteLine("          <Created>2007-11-27T19:36:16Z</Created>")
txtstream.WriteLine("          <Version>12.00</Version>")
txtstream.WriteLine(" </DocumentProperties>")
txtstream.WriteLine(" <ExcelWorkbook        xmlns='urn:schemas-microsoft-
com:office:excel'>")
txtstream.WriteLine("          <WindowHeight>11835</WindowHeight>")
txtstream.WriteLine("          <WindowWidth>18960</WindowWidth>")
txtstream.WriteLine("          <WindowTopX>120</WindowTopX>")
txtstream.WriteLine("          <WindowTopY>135</WindowTopY>")
txtstream.WriteLine("          <ProtectStructure>False</ProtectStructure>")
txtstream.WriteLine("          <ProtectWindows>False</ProtectWindows>")
txtstream.WriteLine(" </ExcelWorkbook>")
txtstream.WriteLine(" <Styles>")
txtstream.WriteLine("          <Style ss:ID='Default' ss:Name='Normal'>")
txtstream.WriteLine("              <Alignment ss:Vertical='Bottom'/>")
txtstream.WriteLine("              <Borders/>")
```

```vb
        txtstream.WriteLine("                        <Font                ss:FontName='Calibri'
x:Family='Swiss' ss:Size='11' ss:Color='#000000'/>")
        txtstream.WriteLine("                    <Interior/>")
        txtstream.WriteLine("                    <NumberFormat/>")
        txtstream.WriteLine("                    <Protection/>")
        txtstream.WriteLine("            </Style>")
        txtstream.WriteLine("            <Style ss:ID='s62'>")
        txtstream.WriteLine("                    <Borders/>")
        txtstream.WriteLine("                        <Font                ss:FontName='Calibri'
x:Family='Swiss' ss:Size='11' ss:Color='#000000' ss:Bold='1'/>")
        txtstream.WriteLine("            </Style>")
        txtstream.WriteLine("            <Style ss:ID='s63'>")
        txtstream.WriteLine("                    <Alignment                ss:Horizontal='Left'
ss:Vertical='Bottom' ss:Indent='2'/>")
        txtstream.WriteLine("                    <Font                ss:FontName='Verdana'
x:Family='Swiss' ss:Size='7.7' ss:Color='#000000'/>")
        txtstream.WriteLine("            </Style>")
        txtstream.WriteLine("    </Styles>")
        txtstream.WriteLine("<Worksheet ss:Name='Process'>")
        txtstream.WriteLine("            <Table    x:FullColumns='1'    x:FullRows='1'
ss:DefaultRowHeight='24.9375'>")
        txtstream.WriteLine("                <Column ss:AutoFitWidth='1' ss:Width='82.5'
ss:Span='5'/>")
        txtstream.WriteLine("    <Row ss:AutoFitHeight='0'>")
        For x = 0 To rs.Fields.Count-1
            txtstream.WriteLine("                    <Cell  ss:StyleID='s62'><Data
ss:Type='String'>" + rs.Fields(x).Name + "</Data></Cell>")
        Next
        txtstream.WriteLine("    </Row>")
        Do While rs.EOF = false
            txtstream.WriteLine("    <Row ss:AutoFitHeight='0' ss:Height='13.5'>")
            For x = 0 To rs.Fields.Count-1
                txtstream.WriteLine("            <Cell><Data ss:Type='String'><![CDATA(" +
str(rs.Fields(x).Value)) + "))></Data></Cell>")
            Next
            txtstream.WriteLine("    </Row>")
            rs.MoveNext()
        Loop
        txtstream.WriteLine("    </Table>")
```

```
txtstream.WriteLine(" <WorksheetOptions          xmlns='urn:schemas-microsoft-
com:office:excel'>")
    txtstream.WriteLine("              <PageSetup>")
    txtstream.WriteLine("                    <Header x:Margin='0.3'/>")
    txtstream.WriteLine("                    <Footer x:Margin='0.3'/>")
    txtstream.WriteLine("                    <PageMargins          x:Bottom='0.75'
x:Left='0.7' x:Right='0.7' x:Top='0.75'/>")
    txtstream.WriteLine("              </PageSetup>")
    txtstream.WriteLine("          <Unsynced/>")
    txtstream.WriteLine("          <Print>")
    txtstream.WriteLine("                 <FitHeight>0</FitHeight>")
    txtstream.WriteLine("                 <ValidPrinterInfo/>")
    txtstream.WriteLine("
       <HorizontalResolution>600</HorizontalResolution>")
    txtstream.WriteLine("
       <VerticalResolution>600</VerticalResolution>")
    txtstream.WriteLine("              </Print>")
    txtstream.WriteLine("          <Selected/>")
    txtstream.WriteLine("          <Panes>")
    txtstream.WriteLine("                 <Pane>")
    txtstream.WriteLine("                         <Number>3</Number>")
    txtstream.WriteLine("                         <ActiveRow>9</ActiveRow>")
    txtstream.WriteLine("                         <ActiveCol>7</ActiveCol>")
    txtstream.WriteLine("                 </Pane>")
    txtstream.WriteLine("          </Panes>")
    txtstream.WriteLine("          <ProtectObjects>False</ProtectObjects>")
    txtstream.WriteLine("          <ProtectScenarios>False</ProtectScenarios>")
    txtstream.WriteLine(" </WorksheetOptions>")
    txtstream.WriteLine("</Worksheet>")
    txtstream.WriteLine("</Workbook>")
    txtstream.Close()
    ws.Run(ws.CurrentDirectory + "\\Products.xml")
```

CREATING XSL FILES

ELOW are examples of creating XSL files.

```
Dim ws As Object = CreateObject("WScript.Shell")
Dim fso As Object = CreateObject("Scripting.FileSystemObject")
Dim    txtstream    As    Object    =fso.OpenTextFile(ws.CurrentDirectory    +
"\Products.xsl", 2, true, -2)
txtstream.WriteLine("<?xml version='1.0' encoding='UTF-8'?>")
txtstream.WriteLine("<xsl:stylesheet                        version='1.0'
xmlns:xsl='http://www.w3.org/1999/XSL/Transform'>")
txtstream.WriteLine("<xsl:template match=""/"">")
txtstream.WriteLine("<html>")
txtstream.WriteLine("<head>")
txtstream.WriteLine("<title>Products</title>")
txtstream.WriteLine("</head>")
#Add Stylesheet Here
txtstream.WriteLine("<body>")
rs.MoveFirst()
```

Single Line Horizontal Reports
```
txtstream.WriteLine("<table border='0' Cellpadding='2' cellspacing='2'>")


txtstream.WriteLine("<tr>")
for x = 0 to rs.Fields.count-1
```

```
        txtstream.WriteLine("<th align='left' nowrap='true'>" + rs.Fields(x).Name
+ "</th>")
    Next
    txtstream.WriteLine("</tr>")
    txtstream.WriteLine("<tr>")
    for x = 0 to rs.Fields.count-1
```

NONE

```
        txtstream.WriteLine("<td><xsl:value-of    select=""data/Products/"    +
rs.Fields(x).Name  + """/></td>")
```

BUTTON

```
        txtstream.WriteLine("<td        align='left'    nowrap='true'><button
style='width:100%;'><xsl:value-of select=""data/Products/" + rs.Fields(x).Name  +
"""/></button></td>")
```

COMBOBOX

```
        txtstream.WriteLine("<td                          align='left'
nowrap='true'><select><option><xsl:attribute        name='value'><xsl:value-of
select=""data/Products/" + rs.Fields(x).Name  + """/></xsl:attribute><xsl:value-of
select=""data/Products/" + rs.Fields(x).Name  + """/></option></select></td>")
```

DIV

```
        txtstream.WriteLine("<td  align='left' nowrap='true'><div><xsl:value-of
select=""data/Products/" + rs.Fields(x).Name  + """/></div></td>")
```

LINK

```
        txtstream.WriteLine("<td      align='left' nowrap='true'><a  href='"  +
rs.Fields(x).Value + "'><xsl:value-of select=""data/Products/" + rs.Fields(x).Name
+ """/></a></td>")
```

LISTBOX

```
        txtstream.WriteLine("<td        align='left'      nowrap='true'><select
multiple><option><xsl:attribute                      name='value'><xsl:value-of
select=""data/Products/" + rs.Fields(x).Name  + """/></xsl:attribute><xsl:value-of
select=""data/Products/" + rs.Fields(x).Name  + """/></option></select></td>")
```

SPAN

```
        txtstream.WriteLine("<td   align='left' nowrap='true'><span><xsl:value-
of select=""data/Products/" + rs.Fields(x).Name  + """/></span></td>")
```

TEXTAREA

```
        txtstream.WriteLine("<td                                    align='left'
nowrap='true'><textarea><xsl:value-of       select=""data/Products/"        +
rs.Fields(x).Name  + """/></textarea></td>")
```

TEXTBOX

```
        txtstream.WriteLine("<td        align='left'     nowrap='true'><input
type='text'><xsl:attribute name=""value""><xsl:value-of select=""data/Products/"
+ rs.Fields(x).Name  + """/></xsl:attribute></input></td>")
    Next
    txtstream.WriteLine("</tr>")
    txtstream.WriteLine("</table>")
    txtstream.WriteLine("</body>")
    txtstream.WriteLine("</html>")
    txtstream.WriteLine("</xsl:template>")
    txtstream.WriteLine("</xsl:stylesheet>")
    txtstream.Close()
```

Multi Line Horizontal Reports

```
txtstream.WriteLine("<table border='0' Cellpadding='2' cellspacing='2>")


        txtstream.WriteLine("<tr>")
```

```
for x = 0 to rs.Fields.count-1
    txtstream.WriteLine("<th>" + rs.Fields(x).Name + "</th>")
Next
txtstream.WriteLine("</tr>")
txtstream.WriteLine("<xsl:for-each select=""data/Products"">")
txtstream.WriteLine("<tr>")
for x = 0 to rs.Fields.count-1
    txtstream.WriteLine("<td><xsl:value-of select="" " + rs.Fields(x).Name + "
""/></td>")
```

NONE

```
    txtstream.WriteLine("<td><xsl:value-of select=""" + rs.Fields(x).Name +
"""/></td>")
```

BUTTON

```
    txtstream.WriteLine("<td          align='left'    nowrap='true'><button
style='width:100%;'><xsl:value-of    select=""" +    rs.Fields(x).Name    +
"""/></button></td>")
```
COMBOBOX

```
    txtstream.WriteLine("<td                                 align='left'
nowrap='true'><select><option><xsl:attribute          name='value'><xsl:value-of
select=""" +    rs.Fields(x).Name    +    """/></xsl:attribute><xsl:value-of
select=""data/Products/" + rs.Fields(x).Name + """/></option></select></td>")
```

DIV

```
    txtstream.WriteLine("<td  align='left' nowrap='true'><div><xsl:value-of
select=""data/Products/" + rs.Fields(x).Name + """/></div></td>")
```

LINK

```
    txtstream.WriteLine("<td     align='left' nowrap='true'><a  href='" +
rs.Fields(x).Value + "'><xsl:value-of select=""data/Products/" + rs.Fields(x).Name
+ """/></a></td>")
```

LISTBOX

```
            txtstream.WriteLine("<td            align='left'    nowrap='true'><select
multiple><option><xsl:attribute                  name='value'><xsl:value-of
select=""data/Products/" + rs.Fields(x).Name  + """/></xsl:attribute><xsl:value-of
select=""data/Products/" + rs.Fields(x).Name  + """/></option></select></td>")
```

SPAN

```
            txtstream.WriteLine("<td   align='left' nowrap='true'><span><xsl:value-
of select=""data/Products/" + rs.Fields(x).Name  + """/></span></td>")
```

TEXTAREA

```
            txtstream.WriteLine("<td                                    align='left'
nowrap='true'><textarea><xsl:value-of        select=""data/Products/"        +
rs.Fields(x).Name  + """/></textarea></td>")
```

TEXTBOX

```
            txtstream.WriteLine("<td           align='left'     nowrap='true'><input
type='text'><xsl:attribute name=""value""><xsl:value-of select=""data/Products/"
+ rs.Fields(x).Name  + """/></xsl:attribute></input></td>")
        Next
        txtstream.WriteLine("</tr>")
        txtstream.WriteLine("</xsl:for-each>")
        txtstream.WriteLine("</table>")
        txtstream.WriteLine("</body>")
        txtstream.WriteLine("</html>")
        txtstream.WriteLine("</xsl:template>")
        txtstream.WriteLine("</xsl:stylesheet>")
        txtstream.Close()
```

Single Line Vertical Reports

```
        for x = 0 to rs.Fields.count-1
```

```
txtstream.WriteLine("<tr><th>" + rs.Fields(x).Name + "</th>")
```

NONE

```
txtstream.WriteLine("<td><xsl:value-of     select=""""data/Products/"     +
rs.Fields(x).Name  + """"/></td></tr>")
```

BUTTON

```
txtstream.WriteLine("<td        align='left'    nowrap='true'><button
style='width:100%;'><xsl:value-of select=""""data/Products/" + rs.Fields(x).Name  +
""""/></button></td></tr>")
```

COMBOBOX

```
txtstream.WriteLine("<td                           align='left'
nowrap='true'><select><option><xsl:attribute        name='value'><xsl:value-of
select=""""data/Products/" + rs.Fields(x).Name  + """"/></xsl:attribute><xsl:value-of
select=""""data/Products/"        +        rs.Fields(x).Name              +
""""/></option></select></td></tr>")
```

DIV

```
txtstream.WriteLine("<td   align='left' nowrap='true'><div><xsl:value-of
select=""""data/Products/" + rs.Fields(x).Name  + """"/></div></td></tr>")
```

LINK

```
txtstream.WriteLine("<td       align='left' nowrap='true'><a  href='"  +
rs.Fields(x).Value + "'><xsl:value-of select=""""data/Products/" + rs.Fields(x).Name
+ """"/></a></td></tr>")
```

LISTBOX

```
txtstream.WriteLine("<td          align='left'     nowrap='true'><select
multiple><option><xsl:attribute                   name='value'><xsl:value-of
select=""""data/Products/" + rs.Fields(x).Name  + """"/></xsl:attribute><xsl:value-of
```

```
select=""""data/Products/"          +          rs.Fields(x).Name                    +
"""/></option></select></td></tr>")
```

SPAN

```
        txtstream.WriteLine("<td   align='left' nowrap='true'><span><xsl:value-
of select=""""data/Products/" + rs.Fields(x).Name  + """/></span></td></tr>")
```

TEXTAREA

```
        txtstream.WriteLine("<td                                          align='left'
nowrap='true'><textarea><xsl:value-of          select=""""data/Products/"          +
rs.Fields(x).Name  + """/></textarea></td></tr>")
```

TEXTBOX

```
        txtstream.WriteLine("<td            align='left'       nowrap='true'><input
type='text'><xsl:attribute name=""""value""""><xsl:value-of select=""""data/Products/"
+ rs.Fields(x).Name  + """/></xsl:attribute></input></td></tr>")
```

```
    Next
    txtstream.WriteLine("</table>")
    txtstream.WriteLine("</body>")
    txtstream.WriteLine("</html>")
    txtstream.WriteLine("</xsl:template>")
    txtstream.WriteLine("</xsl:stylesheet>")
    txtstream.Close()
```

Multi Line Vertical Reports

```
txtstream.WriteLine("<table border='0' Cellpadding='2' cellspacing='2>")
```

```
    for x = 0 to rs.Fields.count-1
        txtstream.WriteLine("<tr><th        align='left'       nowrap='true'>"       +
rs.Fields(x).Name + "</th>")
```

NONE

```
txtstream.WriteLine("<xsl:for-each      select=""data/Products""><td
align='left'  nowrap='true'><xsl:value-of  select="""  +  rs.Fields(x).Name  +
"""/></td></xsl:for-each></tr>")
```

BUTTON

```
txtstream.WriteLine("<xsl:for-each      select=""data/Products""><td
align='left' nowrap='true'><button style='width:100%;'><xsl:value-of select=""" +
rs.Fields(x).Name + """/></button></td></xsl:for-each></tr>")
```

COMBOBOX

```
txtstream.WriteLine("<xsl:for-each      select=""data/Products""><td
align='left'              nowrap='true'><select><option><xsl:attribute
name='value'><xsl:value-of   select="""    +    rs.Fields(x).Name    +
"""/></xsl:attribute><xsl:value-of select=""data/Products/" + rs.Fields(x).Name +
"""/></option></select></td></xsl:for-each></tr>")
```

DIV

```
txtstream.WriteLine("<xsl:for-each      select=""data/Products""><td
align='left'   nowrap='true'><div><xsl:value-of   select=""data/Products/"   +
rs.Fields(x).Name + """/></div></td></xsl:for-each></tr>")
```

LINK

```
txtstream.WriteLine("<xsl:for-each      select=""data/Products""><td
align='left' nowrap='true'><a  href='"  +  rs.Fields(x).Value  +  "'><xsl:value-of
select=""data/Products/"   +   rs.Fields(x).Name   +   """/></a></td></xsl:for-
each></tr>")
```

LISTBOX

```
txtstream.WriteLine("<xsl:for-each          select=""data/Products"""><td
align='left'          nowrap='true'><select          multiple><option><xsl:attribute
name='value'><xsl:value-of  select=""data/Products/"  +  rs.Fields(x).Name  +
""""/></xsl:attribute><xsl:value-of select=""data/Products/" + rs.Fields(x).Name +
""""/></option></select></td></xsl:for-each></tr>")
```

SPAN

```
txtstream.WriteLine("<xsl:for-each          select=""data/Products"""><td
align='left'    nowrap='true'><span><xsl:value-of    select=""data/Products/"    +
rs.Fields(x).Name + """"/></span></td></xsl:for-each></tr>")
```

TEXTAREA

```
txtstream.WriteLine("<xsl:for-each          select=""data/Products"""><td
align='left'  nowrap='true'><textarea><xsl:value-of  select=""data/Products/"  +
rs.Fields(x).Name + """"/></textarea></td></xsl:for-each></tr>")
```

TEXTBOX

```
txtstream.WriteLine("<xsl:for-each          select=""data/Products"""><td
align='left'          nowrap='true'><input          type='text'><xsl:attribute
name=""value""><xsl:value-of  select=""data/Products/"  +  rs.Fields(x).Name  +
""""/></xsl:attribute></input></td></xsl:for-each></tr>")
```

```
      Next
      txtstream.WriteLine("</table>")
      txtstream.WriteLine("</body>")
      txtstream.WriteLine("</html>")
      txtstream.WriteLine("</xsl:template>")
      txtstream.WriteLine("</xsl:stylesheet>")
      txtstream.Close()
```

Single Line Horizontal Tables

```
txtstream.WriteLine("<table        style='border:Double;border-width:1px;border-
color:navy;' rules=all frames=both cellpadding=2 cellspacing=2 Width=0>")
```

```
txtstream.WriteLine("<tr>")
for x = 0 to rs.Fields.count-1
    txtstream.WriteLine("<th align='left' nowrap='true'>" + rs.Fields(x).Name
+ "</th>")

    txtstream.WriteLine("</tr>")
    txtstream.WriteLine("<tr>")
    for x = 0 to rs.Fields.count-1
```

NONE

```
    txtstream.WriteLine("<td><xsl:value-of      select=""data/Products/"      +
rs.Fields(x).Name  + """/></td>")
```

BUTTON

```
    txtstream.WriteLine("<td          align='left'      nowrap='true'><button
style='width:100%;'><xsl:value-of select=""data/Products/" + rs.Fields(x).Name  +
"""/></button></td>")
```

COMBOBOX

```
    txtstream.WriteLine("<td                                    align='left'
nowrap='true'><select><option><xsl:attribute          name='value'><xsl:value-of
select=""data/Products/" + rs.Fields(x).Name  + """/></xsl:attribute><xsl:value-of
select=""data/Products/" + rs.Fields(x).Name  + """/></option></select></td>")
```

DIV

```
    txtstream.WriteLine("<td   align='left' nowrap='true'><div><xsl:value-of
select=""data/Products/" + rs.Fields(x).Name  + """/></div></td>")
```

LINK

```
        txtstream.WriteLine("<td    align='left' nowrap='true'><a href='" +
rs.Fields(x).Value + "'><xsl:value-of select=""data/Products/" + rs.Fields(x).Name
+ """/></a></td>")
```

LISTBOX

```
        txtstream.WriteLine("<td        align='left'    nowrap='true'><select
multiple><option><xsl:attribute            name='value'><xsl:value-of
select=""data/Products/" + rs.Fields(x).Name + """/></xsl:attribute><xsl:value-of
select=""data/Products/" + rs.Fields(x).Name + """/></option></select></td>")
```

SPAN

```
        txtstream.WriteLine("<td   align='left' nowrap='true'><span><xsl:value-
of select=""data/Products/" + rs.Fields(x).Name + """/></span></td>")
```

TEXTAREA

```
        txtstream.WriteLine("<td                                align='left'
nowrap='true'><textarea><xsl:value-of        select=""data/Products/"        +
rs.Fields(x).Name + """/></textarea></td>")
```

TEXTBOX

```
        txtstream.WriteLine("<td        align='left'    nowrap='true'><input
type='text'><xsl:attribute name=""value""><xsl:value-of select=""data/Products/"
+ rs.Fields(x).Name + """/></xsl:attribute></input></td>")

    Next
    txtstream.WriteLine("</tr>")
    txtstream.WriteLine("</table>")
    txtstream.WriteLine("</body>")
    txtstream.WriteLine("</html>")
    txtstream.WriteLine("</xsl:template>")
    txtstream.WriteLine("</xsl:stylesheet>")
    txtstream.Close()
```

Multi Line Horizontal Tables

```
txtstream.WriteLine("<table          style='border:Double;border-width:1px;border-
color:navy;' rules=all frames=both cellpadding=2 cellspacing=2 Width=0>")


    txtstream.WriteLine("<tr>")
    for x = 0 to rs.Fields.count-1
        txtstream.WriteLine("<th>" + rs.Fields(x).Name + "</th>")
    Next
    txtstream.WriteLine("</tr>")
    txtstream.WriteLine("<xsl:for-each select=""data/Products"">")
    txtstream.WriteLine("<tr>")
    for x = 0 to rs.Fields.count-1
        txtstream.WriteLine("<td><xsl:value-of select="" " + rs.Fields(x).Name + "
""/></td>")
```

NONE

```
        txtstream.WriteLine("<td><xsl:value-of select=""""" + rs.Fields(x).Name   +
"""""/></td>")
```

BUTTON

```
        txtstream.WriteLine("<td          align='left'      nowrap='true'><button
style='width:100%;'><xsl:value-of    select="""""   +   rs.Fields(x).Name        +
"""""/></button></td>")
```

COMBOBOX

```
        txtstream.WriteLine("<td                                    align='left'
nowrap='true'><select><option><xsl:attribute          name='value'><xsl:value-of
select="""""   +    rs.Fields(x).Name     +     """""/></xsl:attribute><xsl:value-of
select=""data/Products/" + rs.Fields(x).Name  + """""/></option></select></td>")
```

DIV

```
        txtstream.WriteLine("<td  align='left'  nowrap='true'><div><xsl:value-of
select=""""data/Products/" + rs.Fields(x).Name + """"/></div></td>")
```

LINK

```
        txtstream.WriteLine("<td     align='left'  nowrap='true'><a  href='"  +
rs.Fields(x).Value + "'><xsl:value-of select=""""data/Products/" + rs.Fields(x).Name
+ """"/></a></td>")
```

LISTBOX

```
        txtstream.WriteLine("<td              align='left'      nowrap='true'><select
multiple><option><xsl:attribute                name='value'><xsl:value-of
select=""""data/Products/" + rs.Fields(x).Name + """"/></xsl:attribute><xsl:value-of
select=""""data/Products/" + rs.Fields(x).Name + """"/></option></select></td>")
```

SPAN

```
        txtstream.WriteLine("<td  align='left' nowrap='true'><span><xsl:value-
of select=""""data/Products/" + rs.Fields(x).Name + """"/></span></td>")
```

TEXTAREA

```
        txtstream.WriteLine("<td                            align='left'
nowrap='true'><textarea><xsl:value-of        select=""""data/Products/"        +
rs.Fields(x).Name + """"/></textarea></td>")
```

TEXTBOX

```
        txtstream.WriteLine("<td          align='left'      nowrap='true'><input
type='text'><xsl:attribute name=""""value""""><xsl:value-of select=""""data/Products/"
+ rs.Fields(x).Name + """"/></xsl:attribute></input></td>")

    Next
    txtstream.WriteLine("</tr>")
    txtstream.WriteLine("</xsl:for-each>")
    txtstream.WriteLine("</table>")
```

```
txtstream.WriteLine("</body>")
txtstream.WriteLine("</html>")
txtstream.WriteLine("</xsl:template>")
txtstream.WriteLine("</xsl:stylesheet>")
txtstream.Close()
```

Single Line Vertical Tables

```
for x = 0 to rs.Fields.count-1
    txtstream.WriteLine("<tr><th>" + rs.Fields(x).Name + "</th>")
```

NONE

```
    txtstream.WriteLine("<td><xsl:value-of     select=""data/Products/"     +
rs.Fields(x).Name  + """/></td></tr>")
```

BUTTON

```
        txtstream.WriteLine("<td          align='left'     nowrap='true'><button
style='width:100%;'><xsl:value-of select=""data/Products/" + rs.Fields(x).Name  +
"""/></button></td></tr>")
```

COMBOBOX

```
        txtstream.WriteLine("<td                              align='left'
nowrap='true'><select><option><xsl:attribute          name='value'><xsl:value-of
select=""data/Products/" + rs.Fields(x).Name  + """/></xsl:attribute><xsl:value-of
select=""data/Products/"        +        rs.Fields(x).Name                  +
"""/></option></select></td></tr>")
```

DIV

```
    txtstream.WriteLine("<td   align='left'  nowrap='true'><div><xsl:value-of
select=""data/Products/" + rs.Fields(x).Name  + """/></div></td></tr>")
```

LINK

```
        txtstream.WriteLine("<td    align='left'  nowrap='true'><a  href='" +
rs.Fields(x).Value + "'><xsl:value-of select=""data/Products/" + rs.Fields(x).Name
+ """/></a></td></tr>")
```

LISTBOX

```
        txtstream.WriteLine("<td         align='left'      nowrap='true'><select
multiple><option><xsl:attribute                  name='value'><xsl:value-of
select=""data/Products/" + rs.Fields(x).Name  + """/></xsl:attribute><xsl:value-of
select=""data/Products/"       +        rs.Fields(x).Name              +
"""/></option></select></td></tr>")
```
SPAN

```
        txtstream.WriteLine("<td   align='left' nowrap='true'><span><xsl:value-
of select=""data/Products/" + rs.Fields(x).Name  + """/></span></td></tr>")
```

TEXTAREA

```
        txtstream.WriteLine("<td                              align='left'
nowrap='true'><textarea><xsl:value-of         select=""data/Products/"        +
rs.Fields(x).Name  + """/></textarea></td></tr>")
```

TEXTBOX

```
        txtstream.WriteLine("<td         align='left'     nowrap='true'><input
type='text'><xsl:attribute name=""value""><xsl:value-of select=""data/Products/"
+ rs.Fields(x).Name  + """/></xsl:attribute></input></td></tr>")

    Next
    txtstream.WriteLine("</table>")
    txtstream.WriteLine("</body>")
    txtstream.WriteLine("</html>")
    txtstream.WriteLine("</xsl:template>")
    txtstream.WriteLine("</xsl:stylesheet>")
    txtstream.Close()
```

Multi Line Vertical Tables

txtstream.WriteLine("<table style='border:Double;border-width:1px;border-color:navy;' rules=all frames=both cellpadding=2 cellspacing=2 Width=0>")

for x = 0 to rs.Fields.count-1
    txtstream.WriteLine("<tr><th align='left' nowrap='true'>" + rs.Fields(x).Name + "</th>")

NONE

txtstream.WriteLine("<xsl:for-each select=""data/Products""><td align='left' nowrap='true'><xsl:value-of select=""" + rs.Fields(x).Name + """/></td></xsl:for-each></tr>")

BUTTON

txtstream.WriteLine("<xsl:for-each select=""data/Products""><td align='left' nowrap='true'><button style='width:100%;'><xsl:value-of select=""" + rs.Fields(x).Name + """/></button></td></xsl:for-each></tr>")

COMBOBOX

txtstream.WriteLine("<xsl:for-each select=""data/Products""><td align='left' nowrap='true'><select><option><xsl:attribute name='value'><xsl:value-of select=""" + rs.Fields(x).Name + """/></xsl:attribute><xsl:value-of select=""data/Products/" + rs.Fields(x).Name + """/></option></select></td></xsl:for-each></tr>")

DIV

txtstream.WriteLine("<xsl:for-each select=""data/Products""><td align='left' nowrap='true'> <xsl:value-of select=""data/Products/" + rs.Fields(x).Name + """/> </td></xsl:for-each></tr>")

LINK

```
        txtstream.WriteLine("<xsl:for-each        select=""data/Products""><td
align='left' nowrap='true'><a href='" + rs.Fields(x).Value + "'><xsl:value-of
select=""data/Products/" + rs.Fields(x).Name + """/></a></td></xsl:for-
each></tr>")
```

LISTBOX

```
        txtstream.WriteLine("<xsl:for-each        select=""data/Products""><td
align='left'        nowrap='true'><select        multiple><option><xsl:attribute
name='value'><xsl:value-of select=""data/Products/" + rs.Fields(x).Name +
"""/></xsl:attribute><xsl:value-of select=""data/Products/" + rs.Fields(x).Name +
"""/></option></select></td></xsl:for-each></tr>")
```

SPAN

```
        txtstream.WriteLine("<xsl:for-each        select=""data/Products""><td
align='left' nowrap='true'><span><xsl:value-of select=""data/Products/" +
rs.Fields(x).Name + """/></span></td></xsl:for-each></tr>")
```

TEXTAREA

```
        txtstream.WriteLine("<xsl:for-each        select=""data/Products""><td
align='left' nowrap='true'><textarea><xsl:value-of select=""data/Products/" +
rs.Fields(x).Name + """/></textarea></td></xsl:for-each></tr>")
```

TEXTBOX

```
        txtstream.WriteLine("<xsl:for-each        select=""data/Products""><td
align='left'        nowrap='true'><input        type='text'><xsl:attribute
name=""value""><xsl:value-of select=""data/Products/" + rs.Fields(x).Name +
"""/></xsl:attribute></input></td></xsl:for-each></tr>")
```

```
    Next
    txtstream.WriteLine("</table>")
    txtstream.WriteLine("</body>")
    txtstream.WriteLine("</html>")
    txtstream.WriteLine("</xsl:template>")
```

```
txtstream.WriteLine("</xsl:stylesheet>")
txtstream.Close()
```

STYLESHEETS

Add some Pizzazz To your ASP, HTA, HTML and XSL pages

CSS turns okay into Amazing

ELOW is an assortment of stylesheets. There is nothing spectacular about them Just some ideas you can modify and put your own twist on them.

None

```
txtstream.WriteLine("<style type='text/css'>")
txtstream.WriteLine("th")
txtstream.WriteLine("{")
txtstream.WriteLine("    COLOR: Black;")
txtstream.WriteLine("}")
txtstream.WriteLine("td")
txtstream.WriteLine("{")
txtstream.WriteLine("    COLOR: Black;")
txtstream.WriteLine("}")
txtstream.WriteLine("</style>")
```

Its A Table

```
txtstream.WriteLine("<style type='text/css'>")
txtstream.WriteLine("#itsthetable {")
```

```
txtstream.WriteLine("          font-family: Georgia, """Times New Roman""",
Times, serif;")
txtstream.WriteLine("          color: #036;")
txtstream.WriteLine("}")
txtstream.WriteLine("caption {")
txtstream.WriteLine("          font-size: 48px;")
txtstream.WriteLine("          color: #036;")
txtstream.WriteLine("          font-weight: bolder;")
txtstream.WriteLine("          font-variant: small-caps;")
txtstream.WriteLine("}")
txtstream.WriteLine("th {")
txtstream.WriteLine("          font-size: 12px;")
txtstream.WriteLine("          color: #FFF;")
txtstream.WriteLine("          background-color: #06C;")
txtstream.WriteLine("          padding: 8px 4px;")
txtstream.WriteLine("          border-bottom: 1px solid #015ebc;")
txtstream.WriteLine("}")
txtstream.WriteLine("table {")
txtstream.WriteLine("          margin: 0;")
txtstream.WriteLine("          padding: 0;")
txtstream.WriteLine("          border-collapse: collapse;")
txtstream.WriteLine("          border: 1px solid #06C;")
txtstream.WriteLine("          width: 100%")
txtstream.WriteLine("}")
txtstream.WriteLine("#itsthetable th a:link, #itsthetable th a:visited {")
txtstream.WriteLine("          color: #FFF;")
txtstream.WriteLine("          text-decoration: none;")
txtstream.WriteLine("          border-left: 5px solid #FFF;")
txtstream.WriteLine("          padding-left: 3px;")
txtstream.WriteLine("}")
txtstream.WriteLine("th a:hover, #itsthetable th a:active {")
txtstream.WriteLine("          color: #F90;")
txtstream.WriteLine("          text-decoration: line-through;")
txtstream.WriteLine("          border-left: 5px solid #F90;")
txtstream.WriteLine("          padding-left: 3px;")
txtstream.WriteLine("}")
txtstream.WriteLine("tbody th:hover {")
txtstream.WriteLine("          background-image:
url(imgs/tbody_hover.gif);")
txtstream.WriteLine("          background-position: bottom;")
```

```
txtstream.WriteLine("            background-repeat: repeat-x;")
txtstream.WriteLine("}")
txtstream.WriteLine("td {")
txtstream.WriteLine("            background-color: #f2f2f2;")
txtstream.WriteLine("            padding: 4px;")
txtstream.WriteLine("            font-size: 12px;")
txtstream.WriteLine("}")
txtstream.WriteLine("#itsthetable td:hover {")
txtstream.WriteLine("            background-color: #f8f8f8;")
txtstream.WriteLine("}")
txtstream.WriteLine("#itsthetable td a:link, #itsthetable td a:visited {")
txtstream.WriteLine("            color: #039;")
txtstream.WriteLine("            text-decoration: none;")
txtstream.WriteLine("            border-left: 3px solid #039;")
txtstream.WriteLine("            padding-left: 3px;")
txtstream.WriteLine("}")
txtstream.WriteLine("#itsthetable td a:hover, #itsthetable td a:active {")
txtstream.WriteLine("            color: #06C;")
txtstream.WriteLine("            text-decoration: line-through;")
txtstream.WriteLine("            border-left: 3px solid #06C;")
txtstream.WriteLine("            padding-left: 3px;")
txtstream.WriteLine("}")
txtstream.WriteLine("#itsthetable th {")
txtstream.WriteLine("            text-align: left;")
txtstream.WriteLine("            width: 150px;")
txtstream.WriteLine("}")
txtstream.WriteLine("#itsthetable tr {")
txtstream.WriteLine("            border-bottom: 1px solid #CCC;")
txtstream.WriteLine("}")
txtstream.WriteLine("#itsthetable thead th {")
txtstream.WriteLine("            background-image: url(imgs/thead_back.gif);")
txtstream.WriteLine("            background-repeat: repeat-x;")
txtstream.WriteLine("            background-color: #06C;")
txtstream.WriteLine("            height: 30px;")
txtstream.WriteLine("            font-size: 18px;")
txtstream.WriteLine("            text-align: center;")
txtstream.WriteLine("            text-shadow: #333 2px 2px;")
txtstream.WriteLine("            border: 2px;")
txtstream.WriteLine("}")
txtstream.WriteLine("#itsthetable tfoot th {")
```

```
txtstream.WriteLine("          background-image: url(imgs/tfoot_back.gif);")
txtstream.WriteLine("          background-repeat: repeat-x;")
txtstream.WriteLine("          background-color: #036;")
txtstream.WriteLine("          height: 30px;")
txtstream.WriteLine("          font-size: 28px;")
txtstream.WriteLine("          text-align: center;")
txtstream.WriteLine("          text-shadow: #333 2px 2px;")
txtstream.WriteLine("}")
txtstream.WriteLine("#itsthetable tfoot td {")
txtstream.WriteLine("          background-image: url(imgs/tfoot_back.gif);")
txtstream.WriteLine("          background-repeat: repeat-x;")
txtstream.WriteLine("          background-color: #036;")
txtstream.WriteLine("          color: FFF;")
txtstream.WriteLine("          height: 30px;")
txtstream.WriteLine("          font-size: 24px;")
txtstream.WriteLine("          text-align: left;")
txtstream.WriteLine("          text-shadow: #333 2px 2px;")
txtstream.WriteLine("}")
txtstream.WriteLine("tbody td a(href=""""http://www.csslab.cl/"""") {")
txtstream.WriteLine("          font-weight: bolder;")
txtstream.WriteLine("}")
txtstream.WriteLine("</style>")
```

Black and White Text

```
txtstream.WriteLine("<style type='text/css'>")
txtstream.WriteLine("th")
txtstream.WriteLine("{")
txtstream.WriteLine("   COLOR: white;")
txtstream.WriteLine("   BACKGROUND-COLOR: black;")
txtstream.WriteLine("   FONT-FAMILY: Cambria, serif;")
txtstream.WriteLine("   FONT-SIZE: 12px;")
txtstream.WriteLine("   text-align: left;")
txtstream.WriteLine("   white-Space: nowrap='nowrap';")
txtstream.WriteLine("}")
txtstream.WriteLine("td")
txtstream.WriteLine("{")
txtstream.WriteLine("   COLOR: white;")
txtstream.WriteLine("   BACKGROUND-COLOR: black;")
```

```
txtstream.WriteLine("    FONT-FAMILY: font-family: Cambria, serif;")
txtstream.WriteLine("    FONT-SIZE: 12px;")
txtstream.WriteLine("    text-align: left;")
txtstream.WriteLine("    white-Space: nowrap='nowrap';")
txtstream.WriteLine("}")
txtstream.WriteLine("div")
txtstream.WriteLine("{")
txtstream.WriteLine("    COLOR: white;")
txtstream.WriteLine("    BACKGROUND-COLOR: black;")
txtstream.WriteLine("    FONT-FAMILY: font-family: Cambria, serif;")
txtstream.WriteLine("    FONT-SIZE: 10px;")
txtstream.WriteLine("    text-align: left;")
txtstream.WriteLine("    white-Space: nowrap='nowrap';")
txtstream.WriteLine("}")
txtstream.WriteLine("span")
txtstream.WriteLine("{")
txtstream.WriteLine("    COLOR: white;")
txtstream.WriteLine("    BACKGROUND-COLOR: black;")
txtstream.WriteLine("    FONT-FAMILY: font-family: Cambria, serif;")
txtstream.WriteLine("    FONT-SIZE: 10px;")
txtstream.WriteLine("    text-align: left;")
txtstream.WriteLine("    white-Space: nowrap='nowrap';")
txtstream.WriteLine("    display:inline-block;")
txtstream.WriteLine("    width: 100%;")
txtstream.WriteLine("}")
txtstream.WriteLine("textarea")
txtstream.WriteLine("{")
txtstream.WriteLine("    COLOR: white;")
txtstream.WriteLine("    BACKGROUND-COLOR: black;")
txtstream.WriteLine("    FONT-FAMILY: font-family: Cambria, serif;")
txtstream.WriteLine("    FONT-SIZE: 10px;")
txtstream.WriteLine("    text-align: left;")
txtstream.WriteLine("    white-Space: nowrap='nowrap';")
txtstream.WriteLine("    width: 100%;")
txtstream.WriteLine("}")
txtstream.WriteLine("select")
txtstream.WriteLine("{")
txtstream.WriteLine("    COLOR: white;")
txtstream.WriteLine("    BACKGROUND-COLOR: black;")
txtstream.WriteLine("    FONT-FAMILY: font-family: Cambria, serif;")
```

```
txtstream.WriteLine("    FONT-SIZE: 10px;")
txtstream.WriteLine("    text-align: left;")
txtstream.WriteLine("    white-Space: nowrap='nowrap';")
txtstream.WriteLine("    width: 100%;")
txtstream.WriteLine("}")
txtstream.WriteLine("input")
txtstream.WriteLine("{")
txtstream.WriteLine("    COLOR: white;")
txtstream.WriteLine("    BACKGROUND-COLOR: black;")
txtstream.WriteLine("    FONT-FAMILY: font-family: Cambria, serif;")
txtstream.WriteLine("    FONT-SIZE: 12px;")
txtstream.WriteLine("    text-align: left;")
txtstream.WriteLine("    display:table-cell;")
txtstream.WriteLine("    white-Space: nowrap='nowrap';")
txtstream.WriteLine("}")
txtstream.WriteLine("h1 {")
txtstream.WriteLine("color: antiquewhite;")
txtstream.WriteLine("text-shadow: 1px 1px 1px black;")
txtstream.WriteLine("padding: 3px;")
txtstream.WriteLine("text-align: center;")
txtstream.WriteLine("box-shadow: in2px 2px 5px rgba(0,0,0,0.5), in-2px -
2px 5px rgba(255,255,255,0.5);")
txtstream.WriteLine("}")
txtstream.WriteLine("</style>")
```

Colored Text

```
txtstream.WriteLine("<style type='text/css'>")
txtstream.WriteLine("th")
txtstream.WriteLine("{")
txtstream.WriteLine("    COLOR: darkred;")
txtstream.WriteLine("    BACKGROUND-COLOR: #eeeeee;")
txtstream.WriteLine("    FONT-FAMILY: Cambria, serif;")
txtstream.WriteLine("    FONT-SIZE: 12px;")
txtstream.WriteLine("    text-align: left;")
txtstream.WriteLine("    white-Space: nowrap='nowrap';")
txtstream.WriteLine("}")
txtstream.WriteLine("td")
txtstream.WriteLine("{")
```

```
txtstream.WriteLine("    COLOR: navy;")
txtstream.WriteLine("    BACKGROUND-COLOR: #eeeeee;")
txtstream.WriteLine("    FONT-FAMILY: font-family: Cambria, serif;")
txtstream.WriteLine("    FONT-SIZE: 12px;")
txtstream.WriteLine("    text-align: left;")
txtstream.WriteLine("    white-Space: nowrap='nowrap';")
txtstream.WriteLine("}")
txtstream.WriteLine("div")
txtstream.WriteLine("{")
txtstream.WriteLine("    COLOR: white;")
txtstream.WriteLine("    BACKGROUND-COLOR: navy;")
txtstream.WriteLine("    FONT-FAMILY: font-family: Cambria, serif;")
txtstream.WriteLine("    FONT-SIZE: 10px;")
txtstream.WriteLine("    text-align: left;")
txtstream.WriteLine("    white-Space: nowrap='nowrap';")
txtstream.WriteLine("}")
txtstream.WriteLine("span")
txtstream.WriteLine("{")
txtstream.WriteLine("    COLOR: white;")
txtstream.WriteLine("    BACKGROUND-COLOR: navy;")
txtstream.WriteLine("    FONT-FAMILY: font-family: Cambria, serif;")
txtstream.WriteLine("    FONT-SIZE: 10px;")
txtstream.WriteLine("    text-align: left;")
txtstream.WriteLine("    white-Space: nowrap='nowrap';")
txtstream.WriteLine("    display:inline-block;")
txtstream.WriteLine("    width: 100%;")
txtstream.WriteLine("}")
txtstream.WriteLine("textarea")
txtstream.WriteLine("{")
txtstream.WriteLine("    COLOR: white;")
txtstream.WriteLine("    BACKGROUND-COLOR: navy;")
txtstream.WriteLine("    FONT-FAMILY: font-family: Cambria, serif;")
txtstream.WriteLine("    FONT-SIZE: 10px;")
txtstream.WriteLine("    text-align: left;")
txtstream.WriteLine("    white-Space: nowrap='nowrap';")
txtstream.WriteLine("    width: 100%;")
txtstream.WriteLine("}")
txtstream.WriteLine("select")
txtstream.WriteLine("{")
txtstream.WriteLine("    COLOR: white;")
```

```
txtstream.WriteLine("    BACKGROUND-COLOR: navy;")
txtstream.WriteLine("    FONT-FAMILY: font-family: Cambria, serif;")
txtstream.WriteLine("    FONT-SIZE: 10px;")
txtstream.WriteLine("    text-align: left;")
txtstream.WriteLine("    white-Space: nowrap='nowrap';")
txtstream.WriteLine("    width: 100%;")
txtstream.WriteLine("}")
txtstream.WriteLine("input")
txtstream.WriteLine("{")
txtstream.WriteLine("    COLOR: white;")
txtstream.WriteLine("    BACKGROUND-COLOR: navy;")
txtstream.WriteLine("    FONT-FAMILY: font-family: Cambria, serif;")
txtstream.WriteLine("    FONT-SIZE: 12px;")
txtstream.WriteLine("    text-align: left;")
txtstream.WriteLine("    display:table-cell;")
txtstream.WriteLine("    white-Space: nowrap='nowrap';")
txtstream.WriteLine("}")
txtstream.WriteLine("h1 {")
txtstream.WriteLine("color: antiquewhite;")
txtstream.WriteLine("text-shadow: 1px 1px 1px black;")
txtstream.WriteLine("padding: 3px;")
txtstream.WriteLine("text-align: center;")
txtstream.WriteLine("box-shadow: in2px 2px 5px rgba(0,0,0,0.5), in-2px -
2px 5px rgba(255,255,255,0.5);")
txtstream.WriteLine("}")
txtstream.WriteLine("</style>")
```

Oscillating Row Colors

```
txtstream.WriteLine("<style type='text/css'>")
txtstream.WriteLine("th")
txtstream.WriteLine("{")
txtstream.WriteLine("    COLOR: white;")
txtstream.WriteLine("    BACKGROUND-COLOR: navy;")
txtstream.WriteLine("    FONT-FAMILY: Cambria, serif;")
txtstream.WriteLine("    FONT-SIZE: 12px;")
txtstream.WriteLine("    text-align: left;")
txtstream.WriteLine("    white-Space: nowrap='nowrap';")
txtstream.WriteLine("}")
```

```
txtstream.WriteLine("td")
txtstream.WriteLine("{")
txtstream.WriteLine("    COLOR: navy;")
txtstream.WriteLine("    FONT-FAMILY: font-family: Cambria, serif;")
txtstream.WriteLine("    FONT-SIZE: 12px;")
txtstream.WriteLine("    text-align: left;")
txtstream.WriteLine("    white-Space: nowrap='nowrap';")
txtstream.WriteLine("}")
txtstream.WriteLine("div")
txtstream.WriteLine("{")
txtstream.WriteLine("    COLOR: navy;")
txtstream.WriteLine("    FONT-FAMILY: font-family: Cambria, serif;")
txtstream.WriteLine("    FONT-SIZE: 12px;")
txtstream.WriteLine("    text-align: left;")
txtstream.WriteLine("    white-Space: nowrap='nowrap';")
txtstream.WriteLine("}")
txtstream.WriteLine("span")
txtstream.WriteLine("{")
txtstream.WriteLine("    COLOR: navy;")
txtstream.WriteLine("    FONT-FAMILY: font-family: Cambria, serif;")
txtstream.WriteLine("    FONT-SIZE: 12px;")
txtstream.WriteLine("    text-align: left;")
txtstream.WriteLine("    white-Space: nowrap='nowrap';")
txtstream.WriteLine("    width: 100%;")
txtstream.WriteLine("}")
txtstream.WriteLine("textarea")
txtstream.WriteLine("{")
txtstream.WriteLine("    COLOR: navy;")
txtstream.WriteLine("    FONT-FAMILY: font-family: Cambria, serif;")
txtstream.WriteLine("    FONT-SIZE: 12px;")
txtstream.WriteLine("    text-align: left;")
txtstream.WriteLine("    white-Space: nowrap='nowrap';")
txtstream.WriteLine("    display:inline-block;")
txtstream.WriteLine("    width: 100%;")
txtstream.WriteLine("}")
txtstream.WriteLine("select")
txtstream.WriteLine("{")
txtstream.WriteLine("    COLOR: navy;")
txtstream.WriteLine("    FONT-FAMILY: font-family: Cambria, serif;")
txtstream.WriteLine("    FONT-SIZE: 10px;")
```

```
txtstream.WriteLine("    text-align: left;")
txtstream.WriteLine("    white-Space: nowrap='nowrap';")
txtstream.WriteLine("    display:inline-block;")
txtstream.WriteLine("    width: 100%;")
txtstream.WriteLine("}")
txtstream.WriteLine("input")
txtstream.WriteLine("{")
txtstream.WriteLine("    COLOR: navy;")
txtstream.WriteLine("    FONT-FAMILY: font-family: Cambria, serif;")
txtstream.WriteLine("    FONT-SIZE: 12px;")
txtstream.WriteLine("    text-align: left;")
txtstream.WriteLine("    display:table-cell;")
txtstream.WriteLine("    white-Space: nowrap='nowrap';")
txtstream.WriteLine("}")
txtstream.WriteLine("h1 {")
txtstream.WriteLine("color: antiquewhite;")
txtstream.WriteLine("text-shadow: 1px 1px 1px black;")
txtstream.WriteLine("padding: 3px;")
txtstream.WriteLine("text-align: center;")
txtstream.WriteLine("box-shadow: in2px 2px 5px rgba(0,0,0,0.5), in-2px -
2px 5px rgba(255,255,255,0.5);")
txtstream.WriteLine("}")
txtstream.WriteLine("tr:nth-child(even){background-color:#f2f2f2;}")
txtstream.WriteLine("tr:nth-child(odd){background-color:#cccccc;
color:#f2f2f2;}")
txtstream.WriteLine("</style>")
```

Ghost Decorated

```
txtstream.WriteLine("<style type='text/css'>")
txtstream.WriteLine("th")
txtstream.WriteLine("{")
txtstream.WriteLine("    COLOR: black;")
txtstream.WriteLine("    BACKGROUND-COLOR: white;")
txtstream.WriteLine("    FONT-FAMILY: Cambria, serif;")
txtstream.WriteLine("    FONT-SIZE: 12px;")
txtstream.WriteLine("    text-align: left;")
txtstream.WriteLine("    white-Space: nowrap='nowrap';")
txtstream.WriteLine("}")
```

```
txtstream.WriteLine("td")
txtstream.WriteLine("{")
txtstream.WriteLine("    COLOR: black;")
txtstream.WriteLine("    BACKGROUND-COLOR: white;")
txtstream.WriteLine("    FONT-FAMILY: font-family: Cambria, serif;")
txtstream.WriteLine("    FONT-SIZE: 12px;")
txtstream.WriteLine("    text-align: left;")
txtstream.WriteLine("    white-Space: nowrap='nowrap';")
txtstream.WriteLine("}")
txtstream.WriteLine("div")
txtstream.WriteLine("{")
txtstream.WriteLine("    COLOR: black;")
txtstream.WriteLine("    BACKGROUND-COLOR: white;")
txtstream.WriteLine("    FONT-FAMILY: font-family: Cambria, serif;")
txtstream.WriteLine("    FONT-SIZE: 10px;")
txtstream.WriteLine("    text-align: left;")
txtstream.WriteLine("    white-Space: nowrap='nowrap';")
txtstream.WriteLine("}")
txtstream.WriteLine("span")
txtstream.WriteLine("{")
txtstream.WriteLine("    COLOR: black;")
txtstream.WriteLine("    BACKGROUND-COLOR: white;")
txtstream.WriteLine("    FONT-FAMILY: font-family: Cambria, serif;")
txtstream.WriteLine("    FONT-SIZE: 10px;")
txtstream.WriteLine("    text-align: left;")
txtstream.WriteLine("    white-Space: nowrap='nowrap';")
txtstream.WriteLine("    display:inline-block;")
txtstream.WriteLine("    width: 100%;")
txtstream.WriteLine("}")
txtstream.WriteLine("textarea")
txtstream.WriteLine("{")
txtstream.WriteLine("    COLOR: black;")
txtstream.WriteLine("    BACKGROUND-COLOR: white;")
txtstream.WriteLine("    FONT-FAMILY: font-family: Cambria, serif;")
txtstream.WriteLine("    FONT-SIZE: 10px;")
txtstream.WriteLine("    text-align: left;")
txtstream.WriteLine("    white-Space: nowrap='nowrap';")
txtstream.WriteLine("    width: 100%;")
txtstream.WriteLine("}")
txtstream.WriteLine("select")
```

```
txtstream.WriteLine("{")
txtstream.WriteLine("    COLOR: black;")
txtstream.WriteLine("    BACKGROUND-COLOR: white;")
txtstream.WriteLine("    FONT-FAMILY: font-family: Cambria, serif;")
txtstream.WriteLine("    FONT-SIZE: 10px;")
txtstream.WriteLine("    text-align: left;")
txtstream.WriteLine("    white-Space: nowrap='nowrap';")
txtstream.WriteLine("    width: 100%;")
txtstream.WriteLine("}")
txtstream.WriteLine("input")
txtstream.WriteLine("{")
txtstream.WriteLine("    COLOR: black;")
txtstream.WriteLine("    BACKGROUND-COLOR: white;")
txtstream.WriteLine("    FONT-FAMILY: font-family: Cambria, serif;")
txtstream.WriteLine("    FONT-SIZE: 12px;")
txtstream.WriteLine("    text-align: left;")
txtstream.WriteLine("    display:table-cell;")
txtstream.WriteLine("    white-Space: nowrap='nowrap';")
txtstream.WriteLine("}")
txtstream.WriteLine("h1 {")
txtstream.WriteLine("color: antiquewhite;")
txtstream.WriteLine("text-shadow: 1px 1px 1px black;")
txtstream.WriteLine("padding: 3px;")
txtstream.WriteLine("text-align: center;")
txtstream.WriteLine("box-shadow: in2px 2px 5px rgba(0,0,0,0.5), in-2px -
2px 5px rgba(255,255,255,0.5);")
txtstream.WriteLine("}")
txtstream.WriteLine("</style>")
```

3D

```
txtstream.WriteLine("<style type='text/css'>")
txtstream.WriteLine("body")
txtstream.WriteLine("{")
txtstream.WriteLine("    PADDING-RIGHT: 0px;")
txtstream.WriteLine("    PADDING-LEFT: 0px;")
txtstream.WriteLine("    PADDING-BOTTOM: 0px;")
txtstream.WriteLine("    MARGIN: 0px;")
txtstream.WriteLine("    COLOR: #333;")
```

```
txtstream.WriteLine("    PADDING-TOP: 0px;")
txtstream.WriteLine("    FONT-FAMILY: verdana, arial, helvetica, sans-serif;")
txtstream.WriteLine("}")
txtstream.WriteLine("table")
txtstream.WriteLine("{")
txtstream.WriteLine("    BORDER-RIGHT: #999999 3px solid;")
txtstream.WriteLine("    PADDING-RIGHT: 6px;")
txtstream.WriteLine("    PADDING-LEFT: 6px;")
txtstream.WriteLine("    FONT-WEIGHT: Bold;")
txtstream.WriteLine("    FONT-SIZE: 14px;")
txtstream.WriteLine("    PADDING-BOTTOM: 6px;")
txtstream.WriteLine("    COLOR: Peru;")
txtstream.WriteLine("    LINE-HEIGHT: 14px;")
txtstream.WriteLine("    PADDING-TOP: 6px;")
txtstream.WriteLine("    BORDER-BOTTOM: #999 1px solid;")
txtstream.WriteLine("    BACKGROUND-COLOR: #eeeeee;")
txtstream.WriteLine("    FONT-FAMILY: verdana, arial, helvetica, sans-serif;")
txtstream.WriteLine("    FONT-SIZE: 12px;")
txtstream.WriteLine("}")
txtstream.WriteLine("th")
txtstream.WriteLine("{")
txtstream.WriteLine("    BORDER-RIGHT: #999999 3px solid;")
txtstream.WriteLine("    PADDING-RIGHT: 6px;")
txtstream.WriteLine("    PADDING-LEFT: 6px;")
txtstream.WriteLine("    FONT-WEIGHT: Bold;")
txtstream.WriteLine("    FONT-SIZE: 14px;")
txtstream.WriteLine("    PADDING-BOTTOM: 6px;")
txtstream.WriteLine("    COLOR: darkred;")
txtstream.WriteLine("    LINE-HEIGHT: 14px;")
txtstream.WriteLine("    PADDING-TOP: 6px;")
txtstream.WriteLine("    BORDER-BOTTOM: #999 1px solid;")
txtstream.WriteLine("    BACKGROUND-COLOR: #eeeeee;")
txtstream.WriteLine("    FONT-FAMILY: Cambria, serif;")
txtstream.WriteLine("    FONT-SIZE: 12px;")
txtstream.WriteLine("    text-align: left;")
txtstream.WriteLine("    white-Space: nowrap='nowrap';")
txtstream.WriteLine("}")
txtstream.WriteLine(".th")
txtstream.WriteLine("{")
txtstream.WriteLine("    BORDER-RIGHT: #999999 2px solid;")
```

```
txtstream.WriteLine("    PADDING-RIGHT: 6px;")
txtstream.WriteLine("    PADDING-LEFT: 6px;")
txtstream.WriteLine("    FONT-WEIGHT: Bold;")
txtstream.WriteLine("    PADDING-BOTTOM: 6px;")
txtstream.WriteLine("    COLOR: black;")
txtstream.WriteLine("    PADDING-TOP: 6px;")
txtstream.WriteLine("    BORDER-BOTTOM: #999 2px solid;")
txtstream.WriteLine("    BACKGROUND-COLOR: #eeeeee;")
txtstream.WriteLine("    FONT-FAMILY: font-family: Cambria, serif;")
txtstream.WriteLine("    FONT-SIZE: 10px;")
txtstream.WriteLine("    text-align: right;")
txtstream.WriteLine("    white-Space: nowrap='nowrap';")
txtstream.WriteLine("}")
txtstream.WriteLine("td")
txtstream.WriteLine("{")
txtstream.WriteLine("    BORDER-RIGHT: #999999 3px solid;")
txtstream.WriteLine("    PADDING-RIGHT: 6px;")
txtstream.WriteLine("    PADDING-LEFT: 6px;")
txtstream.WriteLine("    FONT-WEIGHT: Normal;")
txtstream.WriteLine("    PADDING-BOTTOM: 6px;")
txtstream.WriteLine("    COLOR: navy;")
txtstream.WriteLine("    LINE-HEIGHT: 14px;")
txtstream.WriteLine("    PADDING-TOP: 6px;")
txtstream.WriteLine("    BORDER-BOTTOM: #999 1px solid;")
txtstream.WriteLine("    BACKGROUND-COLOR: #eeeeee;")
txtstream.WriteLine("    FONT-FAMILY: font-family: Cambria, serif;")
txtstream.WriteLine("    FONT-SIZE: 12px;")
txtstream.WriteLine("    text-align: left;")
txtstream.WriteLine("    white-Space: nowrap='nowrap';")
txtstream.WriteLine("}")
txtstream.WriteLine("div")
txtstream.WriteLine("{")
txtstream.WriteLine("    BORDER-RIGHT: #999999 3px solid;")
txtstream.WriteLine("    PADDING-RIGHT: 6px;")
txtstream.WriteLine("    PADDING-LEFT: 6px;")
txtstream.WriteLine("    FONT-WEIGHT: Normal;")
txtstream.WriteLine("    PADDING-BOTTOM: 6px;")
txtstream.WriteLine("    COLOR: white;")
txtstream.WriteLine("    PADDING-TOP: 6px;")
txtstream.WriteLine("    BORDER-BOTTOM: #999 1px solid;")
```

```
txtstream.WriteLine("   BACKGROUND-COLOR: navy;")
txtstream.WriteLine("   FONT-FAMILY: font-family: Cambria, serif;")
txtstream.WriteLine("   FONT-SIZE: 10px;")
txtstream.WriteLine("   text-align: left;")
txtstream.WriteLine("   white-Space: nowrap='nowrap';")
txtstream.WriteLine("}")
txtstream.WriteLine("span")
txtstream.WriteLine("{")
txtstream.WriteLine("   BORDER-RIGHT: #999999 3px solid;")
txtstream.WriteLine("   PADDING-RIGHT: 3px;")
txtstream.WriteLine("   PADDING-LEFT: 3px;")
txtstream.WriteLine("   FONT-WEIGHT: Normal;")
txtstream.WriteLine("   PADDING-BOTTOM: 3px;")
txtstream.WriteLine("   COLOR: white;")
txtstream.WriteLine("   PADDING-TOP: 3px;")
txtstream.WriteLine("   BORDER-BOTTOM: #999 1px solid;")
txtstream.WriteLine("   BACKGROUND-COLOR: navy;")
txtstream.WriteLine("   FONT-FAMILY: font-family: Cambria, serif;")
txtstream.WriteLine("   FONT-SIZE: 10px;")
txtstream.WriteLine("   text-align: left;")
txtstream.WriteLine("   white-Space: nowrap='nowrap';")
txtstream.WriteLine("   display:inline-block;")
txtstream.WriteLine("   width: 100%;")
txtstream.WriteLine("}")
txtstream.WriteLine("textarea")
txtstream.WriteLine("{")
txtstream.WriteLine("   BORDER-RIGHT: #999999 3px solid;")
txtstream.WriteLine("   PADDING-RIGHT: 3px;")
txtstream.WriteLine("   PADDING-LEFT: 3px;")
txtstream.WriteLine("   FONT-WEIGHT: Normal;")
txtstream.WriteLine("   PADDING-BOTTOM: 3px;")
txtstream.WriteLine("   COLOR: white;")
txtstream.WriteLine("   PADDING-TOP: 3px;")
txtstream.WriteLine("   BORDER-BOTTOM: #999 1px solid;")
txtstream.WriteLine("   BACKGROUND-COLOR: navy;")
txtstream.WriteLine("   FONT-FAMILY: font-family: Cambria, serif;")
txtstream.WriteLine("   FONT-SIZE: 10px;")
txtstream.WriteLine("   text-align: left;")
txtstream.WriteLine("   white-Space: nowrap='nowrap';")
txtstream.WriteLine("   width: 100%;")
```

```
txtstream.WriteLine("}")
txtstream.WriteLine("select")
txtstream.WriteLine("{")
txtstream.WriteLine("   BORDER-RIGHT: #999999 3px solid;")
txtstream.WriteLine("   PADDING-RIGHT: 6px;")
txtstream.WriteLine("   PADDING-LEFT: 6px;")
txtstream.WriteLine("   FONT-WEIGHT: Normal;")
txtstream.WriteLine("   PADDING-BOTTOM: 6px;")
txtstream.WriteLine("   COLOR: white;")
txtstream.WriteLine("   PADDING-TOP: 6px;")
txtstream.WriteLine("   BORDER-BOTTOM: #999 1px solid;")
txtstream.WriteLine("   BACKGROUND-COLOR: navy;")
txtstream.WriteLine("   FONT-FAMILY: font-family: Cambria, serif;")
txtstream.WriteLine("   FONT-SIZE: 10px;")
txtstream.WriteLine("   text-align: left;")
txtstream.WriteLine("   white-Space: nowrap='nowrap';")
txtstream.WriteLine("   width: 100%;")
txtstream.WriteLine("}")
txtstream.WriteLine("input")
txtstream.WriteLine("{")
txtstream.WriteLine("   BORDER-RIGHT: #999999 3px solid;")
txtstream.WriteLine("   PADDING-RIGHT: 3px;")
txtstream.WriteLine("   PADDING-LEFT: 3px;")
txtstream.WriteLine("   FONT-WEIGHT: Bold;")
txtstream.WriteLine("   PADDING-BOTTOM: 3px;")
txtstream.WriteLine("   COLOR: white;")
txtstream.WriteLine("   PADDING-TOP: 3px;")
txtstream.WriteLine("   BORDER-BOTTOM: #999 1px solid;")
txtstream.WriteLine("   BACKGROUND-COLOR: navy;")
txtstream.WriteLine("   FONT-FAMILY: font-family: Cambria, serif;")
txtstream.WriteLine("   FONT-SIZE: 12px;")
txtstream.WriteLine("   text-align: left;")
txtstream.WriteLine("   display:table-cell;")
txtstream.WriteLine("   white-Space: nowrap='nowrap';")
txtstream.WriteLine("   width: 100%;")
txtstream.WriteLine("}")
txtstream.WriteLine("h1 {")
txtstream.WriteLine("color: antiquewhite;")
txtstream.WriteLine("text-shadow: 1px 1px 1px black;")
txtstream.WriteLine("padding: 3px;")
```

```
txtstream.WriteLine("text-align: center;")
txtstream.WriteLine("box-shadow: in2px 2px 5px rgba(0,0,0,0.5), in-2px -
2px 5px rgba(255,255,255,0.5);")
txtstream.WriteLine("}")
txtstream.WriteLine("</style>")
```

Shadow Box

```
txtstream.WriteLine("<style type='text/css'>")
txtstream.WriteLine("body")
txtstream.WriteLine("{")
txtstream.WriteLine("   PADDING-RIGHT: 0px;")
txtstream.WriteLine("   PADDING-LEFT: 0px;")
txtstream.WriteLine("   PADDING-BOTTOM: 0px;")
txtstream.WriteLine("   MARGIN: 0px;")
txtstream.WriteLine("   COLOR: #333;")
txtstream.WriteLine("   PADDING-TOP: 0px;")
txtstream.WriteLine("   FONT-FAMILY: verdana, arial, helvetica, sans-serif;")
txtstream.WriteLine("}")
txtstream.WriteLine("table")
txtstream.WriteLine("{")
txtstream.WriteLine("   BORDER-RIGHT: #999999 1px solid;")
txtstream.WriteLine("   PADDING-RIGHT: 1px;")
txtstream.WriteLine("   PADDING-LEFT: 1px;")
txtstream.WriteLine("   PADDING-BOTTOM: 1px;")
txtstream.WriteLine("   LINE-HEIGHT: 8px;")
txtstream.WriteLine("   PADDING-TOP: 1px;")
txtstream.WriteLine("   BORDER-BOTTOM: #999 1px solid;")
txtstream.WriteLine("   BACKGROUND-COLOR: #eeeeee;")
txtstream.WriteLine("
filter:progid:DXImageTransform.Microsoft.Shadow(color='silver',    Direction=135,
Strength=16)")
txtstream.WriteLine("}")
txtstream.WriteLine("th")
txtstream.WriteLine("{")
txtstream.WriteLine("   BORDER-RIGHT: #999999 3px solid;")
txtstream.WriteLine("   PADDING-RIGHT: 6px;")
txtstream.WriteLine("   PADDING-LEFT: 6px;")
txtstream.WriteLine("   FONT-WEIGHT: Bold;")
```

```
txtstream.WriteLine("    FONT-SIZE: 14px;")
txtstream.WriteLine("    PADDING-BOTTOM: 6px;")
txtstream.WriteLine("    COLOR: darkred;")
txtstream.WriteLine("    LINE-HEIGHT: 14px;")
txtstream.WriteLine("    PADDING-TOP: 6px;")
txtstream.WriteLine("    BORDER-BOTTOM: #999 1px solid;")
txtstream.WriteLine("    BACKGROUND-COLOR: #eeeeee;")
txtstream.WriteLine("    FONT-FAMILY: font-family: Cambria, serif;")
txtstream.WriteLine("    FONT-SIZE: 12px;")
txtstream.WriteLine("    text-align: left;")
txtstream.WriteLine("    white-Space: nowrap='nowrap';")
txtstream.WriteLine("}")
txtstream.WriteLine(".th")
txtstream.WriteLine("{")
txtstream.WriteLine("    BORDER-RIGHT: #999999 2px solid;")
txtstream.WriteLine("    PADDING-RIGHT: 6px;")
txtstream.WriteLine("    PADDING-LEFT: 6px;")
txtstream.WriteLine("    FONT-WEIGHT: Bold;")
txtstream.WriteLine("    PADDING-BOTTOM: 6px;")
txtstream.WriteLine("    COLOR: black;")
txtstream.WriteLine("    PADDING-TOP: 6px;")
txtstream.WriteLine("    BORDER-BOTTOM: #999 2px solid;")
txtstream.WriteLine("    BACKGROUND-COLOR: #eeeeee;")
txtstream.WriteLine("    FONT-FAMILY: font-family: Cambria, serif;")
txtstream.WriteLine("    FONT-SIZE: 10px;")
txtstream.WriteLine("    text-align: right;")
txtstream.WriteLine("    white-Space: nowrap='nowrap';")
txtstream.WriteLine("}")
txtstream.WriteLine("td")
txtstream.WriteLine("{")
txtstream.WriteLine("    BORDER-RIGHT: #999999 3px solid;")
txtstream.WriteLine("    PADDING-RIGHT: 6px;")
txtstream.WriteLine("    PADDING-LEFT: 6px;")
txtstream.WriteLine("    FONT-WEIGHT: Normal;")
txtstream.WriteLine("    PADDING-BOTTOM: 6px;")
txtstream.WriteLine("    COLOR: navy;")
txtstream.WriteLine("    LINE-HEIGHT: 14px;")
txtstream.WriteLine("    PADDING-TOP: 6px;")
txtstream.WriteLine("    BORDER-BOTTOM: #999 1px solid;")
txtstream.WriteLine("    BACKGROUND-COLOR: #eeeeee;")
```

```
txtstream.WriteLine("    FONT-FAMILY: font-family: Cambria, serif;")
txtstream.WriteLine("    FONT-SIZE: 12px;")
txtstream.WriteLine("    text-align: left;")
txtstream.WriteLine("    white-Space: nowrap='nowrap';")
txtstream.WriteLine("}")
txtstream.WriteLine("div")
txtstream.WriteLine("{")
txtstream.WriteLine("    BORDER-RIGHT: #999999 3px solid;")
txtstream.WriteLine("    PADDING-RIGHT: 6px;")
txtstream.WriteLine("    PADDING-LEFT: 6px;")
txtstream.WriteLine("    FONT-WEIGHT: Normal;")
txtstream.WriteLine("    PADDING-BOTTOM: 6px;")
txtstream.WriteLine("    COLOR: white;")
txtstream.WriteLine("    PADDING-TOP: 6px;")
txtstream.WriteLine("    BORDER-BOTTOM: #999 1px solid;")
txtstream.WriteLine("    BACKGROUND-COLOR: navy;")
txtstream.WriteLine("    FONT-FAMILY: font-family: Cambria, serif;")
txtstream.WriteLine("    FONT-SIZE: 10px;")
txtstream.WriteLine("    text-align: left;")
txtstream.WriteLine("    white-Space: nowrap='nowrap';")
txtstream.WriteLine("}")
txtstream.WriteLine("span")
txtstream.WriteLine("{")
txtstream.WriteLine("    BORDER-RIGHT: #999999 3px solid;")
txtstream.WriteLine("    PADDING-RIGHT: 3px;")
txtstream.WriteLine("    PADDING-LEFT: 3px;")
txtstream.WriteLine("    FONT-WEIGHT: Normal;")
txtstream.WriteLine("    PADDING-BOTTOM: 3px;")
txtstream.WriteLine("    COLOR: white;")
txtstream.WriteLine("    PADDING-TOP: 3px;")
txtstream.WriteLine("    BORDER-BOTTOM: #999 1px solid;")
txtstream.WriteLine("    BACKGROUND-COLOR: navy;")
txtstream.WriteLine("    FONT-FAMILY: font-family: Cambria, serif;")
txtstream.WriteLine("    FONT-SIZE: 10px;")
txtstream.WriteLine("    text-align: left;")
txtstream.WriteLine("    white-Space: nowrap='nowrap';")
txtstream.WriteLine("    display: inline-block;")
txtstream.WriteLine("    width: 100%;")
txtstream.WriteLine("}")
txtstream.WriteLine("textarea")
```

```
txtstream.WriteLine("{")
txtstream.WriteLine("    BORDER-RIGHT: #999999 3px solid;")
txtstream.WriteLine("    PADDING-RIGHT: 3px;")
txtstream.WriteLine("    PADDING-LEFT: 3px;")
txtstream.WriteLine("    FONT-WEIGHT: Normal;")
txtstream.WriteLine("    PADDING-BOTTOM: 3px;")
txtstream.WriteLine("    COLOR: white;")
txtstream.WriteLine("    PADDING-TOP: 3px;")
txtstream.WriteLine("    BORDER-BOTTOM: #999 1px solid;")
txtstream.WriteLine("    BACKGROUND-COLOR: navy;")
txtstream.WriteLine("    FONT-FAMILY: font-family: Cambria, serif;")
txtstream.WriteLine("    FONT-SIZE: 10px;")
txtstream.WriteLine("    text-align: left;")
txtstream.WriteLine("    white-Space: nowrap='nowrap';")
txtstream.WriteLine("    width: 100%;")
txtstream.WriteLine("}")
txtstream.WriteLine("select")
txtstream.WriteLine("{")
txtstream.WriteLine("    BORDER-RIGHT: #999999 3px solid;")
txtstream.WriteLine("    PADDING-RIGHT: 6px;")
txtstream.WriteLine("    PADDING-LEFT: 6px;")
txtstream.WriteLine("    FONT-WEIGHT: Normal;")
txtstream.WriteLine("    PADDING-BOTTOM: 6px;")
txtstream.WriteLine("    COLOR: white;")
txtstream.WriteLine("    PADDING-TOP: 6px;")
txtstream.WriteLine("    BORDER-BOTTOM: #999 1px solid;")
txtstream.WriteLine("    BACKGROUND-COLOR: navy;")
txtstream.WriteLine("    FONT-FAMILY: font-family: Cambria, serif;")
txtstream.WriteLine("    FONT-SIZE: 10px;")
txtstream.WriteLine("    text-align: left;")
txtstream.WriteLine("    white-Space: nowrap='nowrap';")
txtstream.WriteLine("    width: 100%;")
txtstream.WriteLine("}")
txtstream.WriteLine("input")
txtstream.WriteLine("{")
txtstream.WriteLine("    BORDER-RIGHT: #999999 3px solid;")
txtstream.WriteLine("    PADDING-RIGHT: 3px;")
txtstream.WriteLine("    PADDING-LEFT: 3px;")
txtstream.WriteLine("    FONT-WEIGHT: Bold;")
txtstream.WriteLine("    PADDING-BOTTOM: 3px;")
```

```
txtstream.WriteLine("    COLOR: white;")
txtstream.WriteLine("    PADDING-TOP: 3px;")
txtstream.WriteLine("    BORDER-BOTTOM: #999 1px solid;")
txtstream.WriteLine("    BACKGROUND-COLOR: navy;")
txtstream.WriteLine("    FONT-FAMILY: font-family: Cambria, serif;")
txtstream.WriteLine("    FONT-SIZE: 12px;")
txtstream.WriteLine("    text-align: left;")
txtstream.WriteLine("    display: table-cell;")
txtstream.WriteLine("    white-Space: nowrap='nowrap';")
txtstream.WriteLine("    width: 100%;")
txtstream.WriteLine("}")
txtstream.WriteLine("h1 {")
txtstream.WriteLine("color: antiquewhite;")
txtstream.WriteLine("text-shadow: 1px 1px 1px black;")
txtstream.WriteLine("padding: 3px;")
txtstream.WriteLine("text-align: center;")
txtstream.WriteLine("box-shadow: in2px 2px 5px rgba(0,0,0,0.5), in-2px -2px 5px rgba(255,255,255,0.5);")
txtstream.WriteLine("}")
txtstream.WriteLine("</style>")
```

www.ingramcontent.com/pod-product-compliance
Lightning Source LLC
LaVergne TN
LVHW051247050326
832903LV00028B/2612

9 7 8 1 7 2 0 5 1 9 8 7 4